Good Housekeeping

100 Best Chicken
Recipes

HEARST BOOKS

A Division of Sterling Publishing, Co., Inc.
New York

Ellen Levine	Editor in Chief
Susan Westmoreland	Food Director
Susan Deborah Goldsmith	Associate Food Director
Delia Hammock	Nutrition Director
Sharon Franke	Food Appliances Director
Richard Eisenberg	Special Projects Director
Marilu Lopez	Design Director

Supplemental text by Brenda Goldberg
Book Design by Richard Oriolo

10 9 8 7 6 5 4 3 2 1

Published by Hearst Books
A Division of Sterling Publishing Co., Inc.
387 Park Avenue South, New York, NY 10016

Good Housekeeping is a trademark of Hearst Communications, Inc.

The Good Housekeeping Cookbook Seal guarantees that the recipes in this cookbook meet the strict standards of the Good Housekeeping Institute, a source of reliable information and a consumer advocate since 1900. Every recipe has been triple-tested for ease, reliability, and great taste.

www.goodhousekeeping.com

For information about custom editions, special sales, premium and corporate purchases, please contact Sterling Special Sales Department at 800-805-5489 or specialsales@sterlingpub.com.

Manufactured in China

Scholastic Edition

ISBN-13: 978-1-58816-592-3
ISBN-10: 1-58816-592-2

Contents

South-of-the-Border Chicken Soup

Foreword

If, like many families, you're already preparing chicken a couple of nights a week, you'll welcome new inspiration for this versatile favorite. One of the wonderful things about cooking chicken is that it is a succulent canvas for just about any mix of ethnic flavors, herbs, and spices. And the poultry industry has responded to the call for more convenient cuts and preparations. Whether you want to stir-fry chicken tenders, braise bone-in thighs, or sauté breast cutlets, these cuts are in the meat case. All this and a great nutrition profile, too—it's no wonder that chicken is the most often cooked main dish on American dinner tables.

In this volume of the *100 Best Good Housekeeping Recipes* series, you'll find roast chickens from a simply flavored version with lemon and rosemary to a complete meal with roasted vegetables. For nights when you want to have dinner on the table in under half an hour, turn to the chapter on stir-fries and sautés where you'll find Chicken Breasts a l'Orange ready in 20 minutes with the help of a bit of marmalade and a splash of wine vinegar. If your family's tastes run to Asian, try the Peanut-Chicken Stir-Fry—it's child-approved in my house.

Whatever the occasion, you'll find that you don't need tons of time to feed your family a satisfying meal. And as always, each recipe has been triple tested in the *Good Housekeeping* kitchens to ensure delicious results every time.

Susan Westmoreland
Food Director, *Good Housekeeping*

Double-Dipped Potato Chip Chicken

Introduction

All around the globe, chicken has found its way into just about every kitchen. It's no wonder; chicken is healthy, easy to prepare, economical, and best of all versatile. On average, Americans consume more than 75 pounds of chicken per person each year. Favorite family recipes abound. Here we offer over one hundred of our favorites to help you expand your repertoire.

BUYING

Choose fresh, whole birds that appear plump and have meaty breasts (meatier birds are a better buy, because you're paying for less bone per pound). Chicken parts should also look plump. Skin should be smooth and moist and free of bruises and pinfeathers. The color of the skin can range from creamy white to yellow. It simply depends on the bird's feed and breed and is not an indication of flavor or quality. Generally, tenderness depends on the age of the bird. Broiler-fryers are tender young birds that can be roasted, fried, sautéed, grilled, or broiled. Roasting chickens are bred to be large (about 5 to 7 pounds) but are still relatively tender and are best when roasted.

Buy fresh chicken by the "sell-by" date on the package. Once you get the bird home, cook it within two days. When you open the package, you may notice an off odor. Meat is chemically active, and as it ages, it releases sulfur. If the packaging doesn't have air holes, you may notice the accumulated sulfur, but it will quickly disperse into the air. However, if the chicken still smells bad after a couple of minutes, the problem is bacterial spoilage or rancidity or both. Return the chicken to the store.

HANDLING AND STORAGE

Store raw chicken in its original package on a plate to contain any leaks or drips. If wrapped in butcher paper, remove the paper and place the bird in a large plastic bag. Keep chicken in the coldest part of the refrigerator, away from cooked or ready-to-eat foods. Before cooking, pat whole chicken inside and out with paper towels. Don't discard the giblets! Use to make an easy broth or cook, chop, and add to your favorite gravy.

Be sure to wash your hands, the cutting board, and any utensils that have come in contact with raw chicken with hot water and soap. To destroy bacteria, bleach the cutting board with a solution of 1 tablespoon chlorine bleach to 1 gallon warm water.

Freeze raw whole chicken or parts for up to six months. Cool cooked chicken as quickly as possible, then cover and refrigerate for two to three days, or wrap and freeze for up to three months.

THAWING

For safety's sake, it's important to thaw chicken in one of two ways: in the refrigerator or immersed (in its plastic wrapper) in cold water. Never thaw chicken on the kitchen counter, because bacteria can multiply rapidly at room temperature. Here are some tips for successful thawing:

- Frozen chicken should be thawed completely before being cooked, so allow sufficient time, about 4 hours per pound.

- Remove giblets as soon as possible during thawing, then wrap and refrigerate to use in stock or gravy, if desired.

- If the ice crystals have disappeared from the body cavity, the meat is soft, and the joints are flexible, the chicken is thawed.

- Once thawed, cook the chicken within twelve hours. Wipe the body and neck cavities with paper towels and pat the skin dry.

- For reasons of texture, not safety, do not refreeze chicken once it has been thawed.

THE WHITE AND THE DARK OF IT

The breast is the tenderest part of the bird—and the leanest. A $3^1/2$-ounce portion of breast meat without skin has about 4 grams of fat. The same amount of skinless dark meat has about 10 grams of fat. Removing chicken skin slashes the amount of fat almost in half. You may prefer, however, to cook chicken with the skin on to keep the moisture in. Then simply remove the skin before eating. The fat reduction is practically the same.

White meat is ideal for stir-frying, pan-frying, and other quick, moist-cooking methods like poaching. It also takes well to dry-heat methods such as broiling or grilling, but because white meat dries out quickly, care must be taken not to overcook it. Dark meat, on the other hand, really comes into its own in long-simmered casseroles and stews. Boneless thighs and breasts are convenient and also cook quickly. While it's true that chicken cooked on the bone has the best flavor and tends to be juicer, creative seasoning and marinades can add flavor and moisture to these boneless cuts.

ROASTING A PERFECT BIRD

Everyone loves a golden brown bird bursting with flavorful juices. Estimate the roasting time as follows:

ROASTING TIMES

POULTRY	READY-TO-COOK	COOKING TIME (UNSTUFFED)	COOKING TIME (STUFFED)
Chicken (at 350°F)	$2^1/2$ to 3 pounds	$1^1/4$ to $1^1/2$ hours	$1^1/4$ to $1^1/2$ hours
	3 to $4^1/2$ pounds	$1^1/2$ to $1^3/4$ hours	$1^1/2$ to $1^3/4$ hours
	5 to 7 pounds	2 to $2^1/4$ hours	2 to $2^1/4$ hours
Capon (at 325°F)	5 to 6 pounds	2 to $2^1/2$ hours	$2^1/2$ to 3 hours
	6 to 8 pounds	$2^1/2$ to $3^1/2$ hours	3 to 4 hours

The indicated roasting times are only estimates, as there are many variables that affect total cooking time: the temperature of the bird when removed from the refrigerator, the shape of the bird, and the true oven temperature.

Roast the chicken on a rack in the roasting pan to allow the heat to circulate under the bird. If you like, occasionally baste with the pan drippings. Basting doesn't make meat moister, but it does help to crisp and brown the skin. If the skin begins to brown too quickly, cover the bird with a loose tent of foil.

To be sure that a whole chicken is fully cooked, always use a meat thermometer. Insert the thermometer into the thickest part of the thigh just under the drumstick, pointing toward the body. Do not let the thermometer touch any bone. This would give an inaccurate reading, since the bone conducts heat. If you have a standard meat thermometer, insert it before cooking. If you have an instant-read thermometer, use it to test the temperature during the last quarter of the estimated roasting time, removing and washing it after each test. As a second criterion for doneness, insert the tip of a small knife into the thickest part of the thigh. The juices should run clear with no trace of pink. Also check that the legs move easily: Do not cook the bird until the drumsticks "jiggle," or it will be overcooked. Transfer the chicken to a warm platter and let the pan juices stand for a minute, the spoon off most or all of the fat from the top. The degreased juices can be used to make gravy or can be spooned over each serving as a simple but flavorful sauce.

CARVING TIPS
Letting the chicken rest after roasting results in firmer, juicier meat that is easier to carve. Chicken should stand at least ten minutes before carving so the simmmering juices can relax back into the meat. When carving, use a sharp-bladed, thin knife.

Roasts

Mahogany Roast Chicken
recipe on page 12

Mahogany Roast Chicken

Give your roast chicken a deep amber glaze by brushing it with a simple mix of balsamic vinegar, brown sugar, and dry vermouth.

PREP 10 minutes **ROAST** 1 hour 15 minutes **MAKES** 4 main-dish servings.

1 chicken (3½ pounds)	2 tablespoons dark brown sugar
¾ teaspoon salt	2 tablespoons balsamic vinegar
½ teaspoon coarsely ground black pepper	2 tablespoons dry vermouth
	¼ cup water

1. Preheat oven to 375°F. Remove giblets and neck from chicken; reserve for another use. Rinse chicken inside and out with cold running water; drain. Pat dry with paper towels. Sprinkle salt and pepper on outside of chicken. With breast side up, lift wings up toward neck, then fold wing tips under back so wings stay in place. Tie legs together with string.

2. Place chicken, breast side up, on rack in small roasting pan (13" by 9"). Roast chicken 45 minutes.

3. Meanwhile, prepare glaze: In small bowl, stir brown sugar, vinegar, and vermouth until sugar has dissolved.

4. After chicken has roasted 45 minutes, brush with some glaze. Turn oven control to 400°F and roast chicken, brushing with glaze twice more during roasting, until chicken is deep brown, about 30 minutes longer. Chicken is done when temperature on meat thermometer inserted in thickest part of thigh, next to body, reaches 175° to 180°F and juices run clear when thigh is pierced with tip of knife. Transfer chicken to warm platter; let stand 10 minutes to set juices for easier carving.

5. Meanwhile, remove rack from roasting pan. Skim and discard fat from drippings in pan. Add water to pan; heat to boiling over medium heat, stirring until browned bits are loosened from bottom of pan. Serve chicken with pan juices.

EACH SERVING WITH SKIN About 446 calories | 48g protein | 7g carbohydrate | 24g total fat (7g saturated) | 154mg cholesterol | 583mg sodium.

Roast Chicken with Orange Peel and Bay Leaves

A compound butter (butter that is mixed with other ingredients) made with grated orange peel, salt, and pepper is rubbed under the skin of the chicken for extra flavor and aroma.

PREP 10 minutes **ROAST** 1 hour **MAKES** 4 main-dish servings.

1 chicken (3¹/₂ pounds)	¹/₂ teaspoon salt
2 tablespoons butter or margarine, softened	¹/₄ teaspoon coarsely ground black pepper
1¹/₂ teaspoons finely grated orange peel	6 bay leaves

1. Preheat oven to 450°F. Remove giblets and neck from chicken; reserve for another use. Rinse chicken inside and out with cold running water; drain. Pat dry with paper towels.

2. In small bowl, stir butter, orange peel, ¹/₄ teaspoon salt, and pepper until blended. With fingertips, gently separate skin from meat on chicken breast and thighs. Rub butter mixture on meat under skin. Place 1 bay leaf under skin of each breast half. Place remaining 4 bay leaves inside cavity of chicken. Sprinkle remaining ¹/₄ teaspoon salt on outside of chicken.

3. With chicken breast side up, lift wings up toward neck, then fold wing tips under back of chicken so wings stay in place. Tie legs together with string. Place chicken, breast side up, on rack in medium roasting pan (14" by 10").

4. Roast chicken about 1 hour. Chicken is done when temperature on meat thermometer inserted in thickest part of thigh, next to body, reaches 175° to 180°F and juices run clear when thigh is pierced with knife.

5. Transfer chicken to warm platter; let stand 10 minutes to set juices for easier carving. Discard bay leaves.

EACH SERVING About 475 calories | 48g protein | 1g carbohydrate | 30g total fat (11g saturated) | 170mg cholesterol | 482mg sodium.

Lemon-Rosemary Roast Chicken

Scented with lemon juice and fresh rosemary, this simple dish is a good choice for beginners.

PREP 10 minutes **ROAST** 1 hour **MAKES** 4 main-dish servings.

1 chicken (3½ pounds)

1 lemon, cut in half

1 bunch rosemary

¾ teaspoon salt

½ teaspoon coarsely ground black pepper

¼ cup chicken broth

1. Preheat oven to 450°F. Remove giblets and neck from chicken; reserve for another use. Rinse chicken inside and out with cold running water; drain. Pat dry with paper towels.

2. Squeeze juice from lemon halves; set juice and lemon halves aside. Reserve 4 rosemary sprigs; chop enough remaining rosemary to equal 1 tablespoon. Place lemon halves and rosemary sprigs inside cavity of chicken.

3. In cup, mix chopped rosemary, ¼ teaspoon salt, and ¼ teaspoon pepper. With fingertips, gently separate skin from meat on chicken breast and thighs. Rub rosemary mixture on meat under skin. Sprinkle remaining ½ teaspoon salt and ¼ teaspoon pepper on outside of chicken.

4. With chicken breast side up, lift wings up toward neck, then fold wing tips under back of chicken so wings stay in place. Tie legs together with string. Place chicken, breast side up, on rack in medium roasting pan (14" by 10"). Pour lemon juice over chicken.

5. Roast chicken about 1 hour. Chicken is done when temperature on meat thermometer inserted in thickest part of thigh, next to body, reaches 175° to 180°F and juices run clear when thigh is pierced with tip of knife. Transfer chicken to warm platter; let stand 10 minutes to set juices for easier carving.

6. Meanwhile, remove rack from roasting pan. Skim and discard fat from drippings in pan. Add broth to pan drippings; heat to boiling over medium heat, stirring to loosen brown bits from bottom of pan. Serve chicken with pan-juice mixture.

EACH SERVING About 425 calories | 48g protein | 1g carbohydrate | 24g total fat (7g saturated) | 154mg cholesterol | 645mg sodium.

Carving a Roast Chicken

To remove the breast meat, using a thin sharp knife, start along one side of the breastbone, cutting down along the rib cage (scraping against the bones as you go), cutting off the breast meat in one piece. Repeat on the other side.

To carve the breast meat, holding the knife at a slight angle, cut the meat crosswise into even slices.

To remove a chicken leg, force it away from the body with a carving fork until it pops out of its socket. Separate the thigh from the body by cutting through the joint. If you like, separate the drumstick from the thigh by cutting through the center joint. Repeat on the other side. To remove the wings, cut through the joints where the wings meet the body.

Molasses Five-Spice Roast Chicken

A mainstay in Chinese cooking, five-spice powder is a combination of cinnamon, cloves, fennel seeds, star anise, and Szechuan peppercorns—a pungent mixture that adds an exotic touch.

PREP 10 minutes **ROAST** 1 hour **MAKES** 4 main-dish servings.

1 chicken (3 ½ pounds)

1½ teaspoons Chinese five-spice powder

3 medium sweet potatoes (8 ounces each)

2 tablespoons dark molasses

2 tablespoons ketchup

1 tablespoon honey

1 tablespoon soy sauce

½ teaspoon salt

1. Preheat oven to 450°F. Remove giblets and neck from chicken; reserve for another use. Rinse chicken inside and out with cold running water; drain. Pat dry with paper towels. Sprinkle ½ teaspoon five-spice powder inside cavity.

2. With breast side up, lift wings up toward neck, then fold wing tips under back of chicken so wings stay in place. Tie legs together with string.

3. Line medium roasting pan (14" by 10") with foil. Place chicken, breast side up, on rack in center of foil-lined pan. Wash and dry potatoes; pierce with fork. Place potatoes around chicken in pan.

4. In cup, combine molasses, ketchup, honey, soy sauce, salt, and remaining 1 teaspoon five-spice powder. Brush half of molasses glaze all over chicken. Cover pan loosely with foil. Roast chicken 30 minutes.

5. Remove foil; brush remaining glaze over chicken. Roast 30 minutes longer. Chicken is done when temperature on meat thermometer inserted in thickest part of thigh, next to body, reaches 175° to 180°F and juices run clear when thigh is pierced with tip of knife.

6. Transfer potatoes to cutting board; keep warm. With tongs, tilt chicken to allow juices from cavity to run into roasting pan. Transfer chicken to warm platter. Let chicken stand 10 minutes to set juices for easier carving.

7. Cut potatoes into ¾-inch-thick slices; arrange on platter with chicken. Skim and discard fat from pan drippings. Serve chicken and potatoes with pan juices.

EACH SERVING About 540 calories | 43g protein | 44g carbohydrate | 20g total fat (6g saturated) | 161mg cholesterol | 775mg sodium.

Roast Chicken with Forty Cloves of Garlic

Slow roasting mellows garlic to a sweet nuttiness. Serve with lots of crusty bread for spreading the extra garlic.

PREP 15 minutes **ROAST** 1 hour **MAKES** 4 main-dish servings.

1 chicken (3 1/2 pounds)

6 thyme sprigs

1/2 teaspoon salt

1/4 teaspoon coarsely ground black pepper

40 garlic cloves (2 heads), loose papery skin discarded but not peeled

1 cup chicken broth

1. Preheat oven to 450°F. Remove giblets and neck from chicken; reserve for another use. Rinse chicken inside and out with cold running water; drain. Pat dry with paper towels.

2. With fingertips, gently separate skin from meat on chicken breast. Place 2 thyme sprigs under skin of each breast half. Place remaining 2 sprigs inside cavity of chicken. Sprinkle salt and pepper on outside of chicken.

3. With chicken breast side up, lift wings up toward neck, then fold wing tips under back so wings stay in place. Tie legs together with string. Place chicken, breast side up, on rack in small roasting pan (13" by 9").

4. Roast chicken 30 minutes. Add garlic cloves to pan; roast about 30 minutes longer. Chicken is done when temperature on meat thermometer inserted in thickest part of thigh, next to body, reaches 175° to 180°F and juices run clear when thigh is pierced with tip of knife. Transfer chicken to warm platter; let stand 10 minutes to set juices for easier carving.

5. Meanwhile, remove rack from roasting pan. With slotted spoon, transfer garlic cloves to small bowl. Skim and discard fat from drippings in pan. Remove and discard skin from 6 garlic cloves; return peeled garlic to roasting pan and add broth. Heat broth mixture to boiling over medium heat, stirring to loosen browned bits from bottom of pan and mashing garlic with back of spoon until well blended.

6. Serve chicken with pan juices and remaining garlic cloves. Remove skin from chicken before eating, if desired.

EACH SERVING WITH SKIN About 501 calories | 50g protein | 11g carbohydrate | 28g total fat (8g saturated) | 157mg cholesterol | 688mg sodium.

EACH SERVING WITHOUT SKIN About 352 calories | 44g protein | 10g carbohydrate | 14g total fat (4g saturated) | 129mg cholesterol | 667mg sodium.

Garlic

Garlic is an indispensable seasoning, enhancing everything from soups to sauces. It's often used raw. Garlic is available year round. When buying, look for firm heads that are heavy for their size, enclosed in dry, papery layers. Do not buy heads that have soft spots or are sprouting. Store at cool room temperature in a well-ventilated area; it will keep for up to one month. Do not refrigerate.

To use, separate the garlic cloves from the head and peel by placing a clove on the work surface and placing the flat side of a large knife on top. Press down on the knife to lightly crush the garlic and remove the peel. When cooking garlic, take care not to let it brown, or it could become bitter.

Roasting garlic turns it into a soft, spreadable paste with a sweet, mellow flavor. Try it the classic way—spread on grilled or toasted country-style bread. Or, do as chefs do: Toss some of the garlic with cooked vegetables or hot pasta, or stir into soups, mashed potatoes, or rice.

Roast Chicken Béarnaise

This dish gets its name from the classic French sauce, containing vinegar, tarragon, shallots, and butter.

PREP 15 minutes **ROAST** 1 hour **MAKES** 4 main-dish servings.

1 chicken (3½ pounds)

1 teaspoon salt

¾ teaspoon coarsely ground black pepper

1 large lemon, cut in half

3 medium shallots

4 sprigs fresh tarragon plus 1 tablespoon chopped fresh tarragon leaves

¼ cup dry white wine

1 teaspoon tarragon vinegar or white wine vinegar

1 tablespoon butter or margarine

1. Preheat oven to 450°F. Remove giblets and neck from chicken; reserve for another use. Rinse chicken inside and out with cold running water; drain. Pat dry with paper towels.

2. Sprinkle ½ teaspoon salt and ¼ teaspoon pepper inside cavity. Squeeze juice from lemon into cavity, then place halves inside cavity. Coarsely chop 2 shallots; add to cavity with tarragon sprigs.

3. With chicken breast side up, lift wing tips up toward neck, then fold wing tips under back of chicken so wings stay in place. Tie legs together with string. Place chicken, breast side up, on rack in medium roasting pan (14" by 10"). Sprinkle remaining ½ teaspoon salt and ¼ teaspoon pepper on outside of chicken.

4. Roast chicken about 1 hour. Chicken is done when temperature on meat thermometer inserted in thickest part of thigh, next to body, reaches 175° to 180°F and juices run clear when thigh is pierced with tip of knife.

5. Finely chop remaining shallot. With tongs, tilt chicken to drain juices from cavity into roasting pan. Transfer chicken to warm platter; let stand 10 minutes to set juices for easier carving.

6. Meanwhile, remove rack from roasting pan. Skim and discard fat from drippings in pan. Add wine, vinegar, and chopped shallot to roasting pan; heat to boiling over high heat, stirring to loosen brown bits from bottom of pan. Remove pan from heat; stir in butter and chopped tarragon. Serve chicken with sauce.

EACH SERVING About 375 calories | **40g protein** | **1g carbohydrate** |
22g total fat (7g saturated) | **164mg cholesterol** | **726mg sodium.**

Storing Fresh Herbs

Most fresh herbs are highly perishable, so buy them in small quantities. To store for a few days, immerse the roots or stems in 2 inches of water. Cover with a plastic bag and refrigerate. If you often use fresh herbs, you might want to invest a few dollars in an herb storage jar specially designed for the purpose.

Roast Peking Chicken

Peking duck is an elaborate Chinese dish in which air is forced between the skin and meat to produce the crispiest skin imaginable. Our twist employs boiling water poured over the chicken which tightens the skin and yields a tender, juicy bird with very crisp skin.

PREP 20 minutes **ROAST** 1 hour **MAKES** 4 main-dish servings.

1 chicken (3½ pounds)

2 tablespoons honey

2 tablespoons soy sauce

1 teaspoon seasoned rice vinegar

1 tablespoon minced, peeled fresh ginger

2 garlic cloves, crushed with garlic press

⅛ teaspoon ground red pepper (cayenne)

8 (8-inch) flour tortillas

¼ cup chicken broth

2 tablespoons water

¼ cup hoisin sauce

2 green onions, each cut crosswise into thirds and sliced lengthwise into thin strips

1. Preheat oven to 450°F. Remove giblets and neck from chicken; reserve for another use. Rinse chicken inside and out with cold running water; drain. Pat dry with paper towels.

2. With chicken breast side up, lift wings up toward neck, then fold wing tips under back of chicken so wings stay in place. Tie legs together with string.

3. Place chicken on rack in sink. With chicken breast side up, slowly pour *1 quart boiling water* over chicken. Turn chicken over; slowly pour additional *1 quart boiling water* over back of chicken. (This process allows fat to render easily from chicken and helps crisp skin during roasting.)

4. Place chicken, breast side up, on rack in small roasting pan (13" by 9"). Roast chicken 50 minutes.

5. Meanwhile, in small bowl, combine honey, soy sauce, vinegar, ginger, garlic, and ground red pepper.

6. After chicken has roasted 50 minutes, brush with half of honey glaze; roast another 5 minutes. Brush with remaining glaze; roast about 5 minutes longer. Chicken is done when temperature on meat thermometer inserted in thickest part of thigh, next to body, reaches 175° to 180°F and juices run clear when thigh is pierced with tip of knife.

7. Transfer chicken to warm platter; let stand 10 minutes to set juices for easier carving.

8. Meanwhile, warm tortillas as label directs. Remove rack from roasting pan. Skim and discard fat from drippings in pan. Add broth and water to pan drippings; heat to boiling over medium heat, stirring until browned bits are loosened from bottom of pan. Stir in hoisin sauce.

9. To serve, slice chicken and wrap in tortillas with hoisin-sauce mixture and green onions.

EACH SERVING WITH SKIN About 739 calories | 55g protein | 59g carbohydrate | 29g total fat (7g saturated) | 154mg cholesterol | 1,401mg sodium.

Chili-Rubbed Roast Chicken with Cherry Tomatoes and Potatoes

Spice rubs are very popular these days and with good reason: They make seasoning poultry or meat quick and easy. Be creative and try experimenting with your own spice mixtures.

PREP 10 minutes **ROAST** 1 hour **MAKES** 4 main-dish servings.

1 chicken (3½ pounds)

2 teaspoons chili powder

1 teaspoon ground cumin

1 teaspoon paprika

1 teaspoon sugar

¼ teaspoon ground red pepper (cayenne)

¾ teaspoon salt

2 medium red onions (1 pound), cut into 1-inch chunks

1 pound red potatoes, cut into 1-inch chunks

1 pint cherry tomatoes

1 tablespoon olive oil

1. Preheat oven to 450°F. Remove giblets and neck from chicken; reserve for another use. Rinse chicken inside and out with cold running water; drain. Pat chicken dry with paper towels.

2. In cup, combine chili powder, cumin, paprika, sugar, ground red pepper, and ½ teaspoon salt. In large roasting pan (17" by 11½"), toss onions, potatoes, and tomatoes with oil and remaining ¼ teaspoon salt until coated. Push vegetables to sides of pan.

3. Rub spice mixture all over chicken. With breast side up, lift wing tips up toward neck, then fold wing tips under back of chicken so wings stay in place. Tie legs together with string.

4. Place chicken, breast side up, on small rack in center of roasting pan. Cover pan loosely with foil. Roast chicken 30 minutes.

5. Remove foil; roast chicken 30 minutes longer. Chicken is done when temperature on meat thermometer inserted in thickest part of thigh, next

to body, reaches 175°F to 180°F and juices run clear when thigh is pierced with tip of knife.

6. Transfer vegetables to warm platter. With tongs, tilt chicken to drain juices from cavity into roasting pan. Transfer chicken to platter with vegetables; let stand 10 minutes to set juices for easier carving.

7. Meanwhile, remove rack from roasting pan. Skim and discard fat from pan drippings. Serve chicken and vegetables with pan juices.

EACH SERVING About 560 calories | 44g protein | 39g carbohydrate |
26g total fat (7g saturated) | 159mg cholesterol | 585mg sodium.

To Skin or Not to Skin

Chicken skin gets 80 percent of its calories from fat, so it makes sense to serve your bird without it. But you don't have to remove the skin before cooking. According to the U.S. Department of Agriculture (USDA), it makes little difference in the fat content whether the skin is removed before or after cooking. But tastewise, especially when roasting whole chicken, you'll get a moister, more tender result if you cook with the skin still intact. If you're watching calories and/or fat grams, the following might serve as a skin-removal incentive: A 3½-ounce cooked serving of chicken breast with skin is about 197 calories with 8 grams of fat; the same serving without skin is only about 165 calories with 4 grams of fat. A drumstick and thigh with skin is about 232 calories with 13 grams of fat; the same serving without skin is about 191 calories with 8 grams of fat.

Roast Chicken with Vegetables

Roasting a whole chicken with sweet potatoes, onion, and an apple means deliciously flavored accompaniments are ready at the same time the chicken is. If you use a larger pan, the vegetables may brown more quickly, so check and remove them when they are tender.

PREP 10 minutes   **ROAST** about 1 hour   **MAKES** 4 main-dish servings.

1 chicken (3½ pounds)

2 medium sweet potatoes (10 ounces each), unpeeled and each cut into 8 wedges

1 jumbo onion (1 pound), cut into 8 wedges

¾ teaspoon salt

¼ teaspoon coarsely ground black pepper

1 Golden Delicious apple, unpeeled, cored, and cut into 8 wedges

2 tablespoons orange marmalade

1. Preheat oven to 450°F. Remove giblets and neck from chicken; reserve for another use. Rinse chicken inside and out with cold running water; drain. Pat dry with paper towels. With chicken breast side up, lift wings up toward neck, then fold wing tips under back of chicken so wings stay in place. Tie legs together with string. Place chicken, breast side up, on rack in medium roasting pan (14" by 10").

2. Place sweet-potato and onion wedges around rack in pan. Rub chicken with ½ teaspoon salt and pepper. Sprinkle vegetables with remaining ¼ teaspoon salt.

3. Roast chicken and vegetables 40 minutes. Remove pan from oven. With tongs, tilt chicken to drain juices from cavity onto vegetables. Add apple wedges to pan. Return pan to oven; roast 15 minutes longer. Brush chicken with marmalade; roast 5 minutes longer. Chicken is done when temperature on meat thermometer inserted in thickest part of thigh, next to body, reaches 175° to 180°F and juices run clear when thigh is pierced with tip of knife.

4. Transfer chicken to warm platter; let stand 10 minutes to set juices for easier carving. Spoon vegetable mixture around chicken.

EACH SERVING WITHOUT SKIN About 470 calories | 39g protein | 47g carbohydrate | 15g total fat (4g saturated) | 113mg cholesterol | 535mg sodium.

Lemon-Fennel Roasted Chicken Pieces

Fennel is available fall through spring. If it is out of season you can substitute celery which becomes sweeter and mellower with roasting.

PREP 20 minutes   **ROAST** 25 minutes   **MAKES** 4 main-dish servings.

1 to 2 lemons

1 tablespoon olive oil

1 teaspoon salt

1/2 teaspoon coarsely ground black pepper

1/2 teaspoon fennel seeds, crushed

1 chicken (3 1/2 pounds), cut into 8 pieces and skin removed

1 large fennel bulb (1 1/2 pounds), trimmed and cut lengthwise into 8 wedges, or 1 celery heart, separated into stalks and cut into 3-inch pieces

1. Preheat oven to 450°F. From lemons, grate 1 teaspoon peel and squeeze 1/4 cup juice. In small bowl, combine oil, salt, pepper, fennel seeds, and lemon peel and juice.

2. Arrange chicken and fresh fennel in large roasting pan (17" by 11 1/2"). Drizzle lemon-juice mixture over chicken and fennel; let stand 15 minutes.

3. Roast chicken and fennel, basting occasionally with pan juices, until juices run clear when chicken is pierced with knife and fennel is fork-tender, 25 to 30 minutes.

4. Transfer chicken and fennel to warm platter. Skim and discard fat from pan drippings. To serve, spoon drippings over chicken.

EACH SERVING About 280 calories | 34g protein | 8g carbohydrate | 12g total fat (3g saturated) | 101mg cholesterol | 725mg sodium.

Thyme-Roasted Chicken and Vegetables

Instead of the traditional combination of carrots, potatoes, and onion, this hearty one-pot meal uses fennel and red onion for a more subtle flavor.

PREP 20 minutes   **ROAST** 50 minutes   **MAKES** 4 main-dish servings.

1 chicken (3½ pounds), cut into 8 pieces and skin removed from all but wings

1 pound all-purpose potatoes (3 medium), not peeled, cut into 2-inch pieces

1 large fennel bulb (1½ pounds), trimmed and cut into 8 wedges

1 large red onion, cut into 8 wedges

1 tablespoon chopped fresh thyme or 1 teaspoon dried thyme

1 teaspoon salt

½ teaspoon ground black pepper

2 tablespoons olive oil

⅓ cup water

1. Preheat oven to 450°F. In large roasting pan (17" by 11½"), arrange chicken, skinned side up, and place potatoes, fennel, and onion around pieces. Sprinkle chicken with thyme, salt, and pepper. Drizzle oil over chicken and vegetables.

2. Roast chicken and vegetables 20 minutes; baste with drippings in pan. Roast, basting once more, until juices run clear when chicken breasts are pierced with tip of knife, about 20 minutes longer. Transfer chicken breasts to platter; keep warm.

3. Continue roasting remaining chicken pieces until juices run clear when thickest part of chicken is pierced with tip of knife and vegetables are fork-tender, about 10 minutes longer. Transfer chicken and vegetables to platter with breasts; keep warm.

4. Skim and discard fat from drippings in pan. Add water to pan drippings; heat to boiling over medium heat, stirring to loosen brown bits from bottom of pan. To serve, spoon pan juices over chicken and vegetables.

EACH SERVING About 401 calories | 43g protein | 28g carbohydrate | 13g total fat (2g saturated) | 124mg cholesterol | 870mg sodium.

Roasted Tandoori-Style Chicken Breasts

A lowfat yogurt marinade packed with spices tenderizes the chicken. Great with rice and grilled onions.

PREP 10 minutes plus marinating **ROAST** 30 minutes **MAKES** 6 main-dish servings.

2 limes

1 container (8 ounces) plain lowfat yogurt

$^1/_2$ small onion, chopped

1 tablespoon minced, peeled fresh ginger

1 tablespoon paprika

1 teaspoon ground cumin

1 teaspoon ground coriander

$^3/_4$ teaspoon salt

$^1/_4$ teaspoon ground red pepper (cayenne)

pinch ground cloves

6 medium bone-in chicken breast halves (3 pounds), skin removed

1. From 1 lime, squeeze 2 tablespoons juice. Cut remaining lime into 6 wedges; set aside for garnish. In blender, puree juice, yogurt, onion, ginger, paprika, cumin, coriander, salt, ground red pepper, and cloves until smooth. Place marinade and chicken in medium bowl or in ziptight plastic bag, turning to coat chicken. Cover bowl or seal bag and refrigerate chicken 30 minutes to marinate.

2. Preheat oven to 450°F. Arrange chicken on rack in medium roasting pan (14" by 10"). Spoon half of marinade over chicken; discard remaining marinade.

3. Roast chicken until juices run clear when thickest part of breast is pierced with tip of knife, about 30 minutes.

4. Transfer chicken to warm platter; garnish with lime wedges to serve.

EACH SERVING About 195 calories | 36g protein | 5g carbohydrate | 3g total fat (1g saturated) | 88mg cholesterol | 415mg sodium.

Lemony Roast Chicken with Artichokes

Cook plump thighs and drumsticks with spring artichokes and baby red potatoes for a delectable dinner. Make sure to use a large roasting pan; otherwise ingredients will steam, not brown.

PREP 30 minutes   **ROAST** 40 minutes   **MAKES** 6 main-dish servings.

3 large lemons

3 garlic cloves, crushed with garlic press

3 tablespoons olive oil

1 $^1/_2$ teaspoons salt

1 teaspoon dried oregano

$^1/_2$ teaspoon coarsely ground black pepper

6 large chicken thighs (1$^3/_4$ pounds), skin and fat removed

6 medium chicken drumsticks (1 $^1/_2$ pounds), skin removed

2 pounds baby red potatoes, cut in half

4 medium or 16 baby artichokes

1. Preheat oven to 450°F. From 2 lemons, grate 2 teaspoons peel and squeeze $^1/_2$ cup juice. Cut remaining lemon in half.

2. In cup, mix lemon peel, garlic, oil, salt, oregano, and pepper. In large roasting pan (17" by 11$^1/_2$"), toss chicken thighs, drumsticks, and potatoes with oil mixture. Roast 20 minutes.

3. While chicken is roasting, prepare artichokes: From around base of artichoke, bend back outer green leaves and snap off. Cut off stem; peel. Pull dark outer leaves from artichoke bottom. With kitchen shears, trim thorny tops from remaining outer leaves, rubbing all cut surfaces with lemon half to prevent browning. Lay artichoke on its side and cut off stem level with bottom of artichoke; peel stem. Cut 1 inch off top of artichoke, then cut lengthwise into quarters. Scrape out choke, removing center petals and fuzzy center portion; discard. Place artichoke stem and quarters in bowl of cold water with juice of remaining lemon half to prevent browning. Repeat with remaining artichokes.

4. In 5-quart saucepot, heat 1 tablespoon lemon juice and *1 inch water* to boiling over medium-high heat. Add artichokes and stems; cook, covered, until fork-tender, about 10 minutes. Drain well on paper towels.

5. Add artichokes to roasting pan with chicken and roast until juices run clear when thickest part of chicken is pierced with tip of knife and potatoes are tender, about 20 minutes longer.

6. Pour remaining lemon juice over chicken and vegetables; toss. To serve, transfer chicken and vegetables to large serving bowl.

EACH SERVING **About 385 calories** I **34g protein** I **36g carbohydrate** I **12g total fat (2g saturated)** I **111mg cholesterol** I **740mg sodium.**

Pan-Roasted Chicken and Vegetables

Boneless chicken thighs, red potatoes, onion wedges, and spinach are roasted together for an easy and satisfying one-dish meal.

PREP 15 minutes **ROAST** 45 minutes **MAKES** 4 main-dish servings.

1 ½ pounds red potatoes, cut into
1 ½-inch chunks

1 jumbo onion (1 pound), cut into
12 wedges

4 garlic cloves, peeled

2 tablespoons olive oil

1 ¼ teaspoons salt

½ teaspoon ground black pepper

½ teaspoon dried rosemary

1 pound skinless, boneless chicken
thighs, each cut into quarters

1 bag (10 ounces) spinach,
stems discarded

1. Preheat oven to 475°F. In large roasting pan (17" by 11½"), combine potatoes, onion, garlic, oil, salt, pepper, and rosemary; toss to coat.

2. Roast vegetables, stirring once, 25 minutes. Add chicken; toss to coat. Roast until juices run clear when thickest piece of chicken is pierced with tip of knife, about 15 minutes longer.

3. Place spinach over chicken mixture and roast until spinach wilts, about 5 minutes longer. Toss before serving.

EACH SERVING About 440 calories | 34g protein | 48g carbohydrate |
13g total fat (2g saturated) | 118mg cholesterol | 930mg sodium.

Braises & Stews

Creole Chicken Gumbo
recipe on page 52

Coq au Vin

This well-known dish—chicken, mushrooms, and pearl onions stewed in red-wine—is a specialty of the Burgundy region of France. Use a moderately priced California or Oregon Pinot Noir, which is made from the same grape as more expensive French Burgundy.

PREP 45 minutes **BAKE** 45 minutes **MAKES** 6 main-dish servings.

4 slices bacon, cut into ³/₄-inch pieces

4 tablespoons butter or margarine

I chicken (3¹/₂ pounds), cut into 8 pieces and skin removed from all but wings

¹/₄ teaspoon salt

¹/₈ teaspoon ground black pepper

I small onion, finely chopped

I carrot, peeled and finely chopped

18 pearl onions (generous I cup), peeled

10 ounces mushrooms, trimmed

¹/₃ cup all-purpose flour

2 cups dry red wine

1¹/₃ cups chicken broth

2 tablespoons tomato paste

I stalk celery

12 sprigs plus 3 tablespoons chopped fresh parsley

2 bay leaves

I. Preheat oven to 325°F. In 5-quart Dutch oven, cook bacon over medium-high heat until crisp. With slotted spoon, transfer to paper towels to drain. Reduce heat to medium and add butter to drippings in pot. Sprinkle chicken with salt and pepper. Add chicken to Dutch oven, in batches if necessary, and cook until golden brown, about 5 minutes per side. With slotted spoon, transfer chicken pieces to bowl as they are browned.

2. Add chopped onion and carrot to Dutch oven and cook until lightly browned, about 5 minutes. With slotted spoon, transfer to bowl with chicken. Add pearl onions to Dutch oven and cook, stirring, until browned, about 6 minutes; transfer to bowl. Add mushrooms to pot and cook, stirring, until browned, about 6 minutes; transfer to bowl.

3. Add flour to Dutch oven and cook, stirring, 2 minutes. With wire whisk, whisk in ¹/₂ cup wine until smooth. Add remaining 1¹/₂ cups wine, broth, and tomato paste. Heat to boiling, whisking constantly; boil 2 minutes. Return chicken, vegetables, and three-fourths of bacon to Dutch oven. Tie celery, parsley sprigs, and bay leaves together; add to Dutch oven. Cover and place in oven. Bake, stirring occasionally, 45 minutes.

4. At end of cooking time, skim fat and discard celery bundle. Sprinkle coq au vin with remaining bacon and chopped parsley.

EACH SERVING About 414 calories | 32g protein | 17g carbohydrate | 24g total fat (10g saturated) | 115mg cholesterol | 645mg sodium.

Chicken Cacciatore

Food prepared *alla cacciatore*, "hunter-style," includes mushrooms in the sauce. This is the kind of Italian home cooking that found its way first into Italian-American restaurants and then into American kitchens. Serve over wide, flat noodles.

PREP 15 minutes   **COOK** 40 minutes   **MAKES** 4 main-dish servings.

2 tablespoons olive oil

1 chicken (3½ pounds), cut into 8 pieces and skin removed from all but wings

3 tablespoons all-purpose flour

1 medium onion, finely chopped

4 garlic cloves, crushed with garlic press

8 ounces mushrooms, trimmed and thickly sliced

1 can (14 to 16 ounces) tomatoes

½ teaspoon salt

½ teaspoon dried oregano, crumbled

¼ teaspoon dried sage

⅛ teaspoon ground red pepper (cayenne)

1. In nonstick 12-inch skillet, heat oil over medium-high heat until very hot. On waxed paper, coat chicken with flour, shaking off excess. Add chicken to skillet and cook until golden brown, about 3 minutes per side. With slotted spoon, transfer chicken pieces to bowl as they are browned.

2. Add onion and garlic to skillet. Reduce heat to medium-low and cook, stirring occasionally, until onion is tender, about 5 minutes. Add mushrooms and cook, stirring frequently, until just tender, about 3 minutes.

3. Add tomatoes with their juice, breaking them up with side of spoon. Add salt, oregano, sage, ground red pepper, and chicken and heat to boiling over high heat. Reduce heat; cover and simmer until chicken loses its pink color throughout, about 25 minutes.

4. Transfer chicken to serving bowl. Spoon sauce over chicken.

EACH SERVING About 371 calories | 44g protein | 18g carbohydrate | 13g total fat (3g saturated) | 133mg cholesterol | 608mg sodium.

Chicken Paprika

For authentic flavor, use sweet Hungarian paprika for this dish. If you can't find it, use regular paprika, not hot, as a substitute.

PREP 15 minutes **COOK** 1 hour 15 minutes **MAKES** 4 main-dish servings.

3 tablespoons vegetable oil

12 ounces medium mushrooms, each cut in half

1 teaspoon salt

3 tablespoons all-purpose flour

3 teaspoons sweet Hungarian paprika

1 chicken (3½ pounds), cut into 8 pieces and skin removed from all but wings

1 medium onion, thinly sliced

1 cup chicken broth

½ cup sour cream

6 ounces wide egg noodles

1. In 12-inch skillet, heat 1 tablespoon oil over medium heat. Add mushrooms and ¼ teaspoon salt and cook until mushrooms are tender and browned and all liquid has evaporated. Transfer mushrooms to large bowl.

2. In large plastic bag, mix flour, 1 teaspoon paprika, and remaining ¾ teaspoon salt. Add chicken pieces and shake to coat with flour mixture (reserve any flour mixture remaining in bag).

3. In same skillet, heat 1 tablespoon oil over medium-high heat until very hot. Add half of chicken pieces at a time and cook until browned. With slotted spoon, transfer chicken to bowl with mushrooms. Add remaining 1 tablespoon oil and onion and cook until tender and lightly browned. Stir in remaining 2 teaspoons paprika and any remaining flour mixture; cook 1 minute. Stir in chicken broth and sour cream.

4. Return mushrooms and chicken to skillet; heat to boiling over high heat. Reduce heat to low; cover and simmer until chicken loses its pink color throughout, about 40 minutes.

5. About 15 minutes before chicken is done, prepare noodles as label directs; drain. To serve, skim fat from liquid in skillet. Spoon the chicken mixture and noodles onto large platter.

EACH SERVING About 610 calories | 51g protein | 45g carbohydrate | 25g total fat (7g saturated) | 3g fiber | 187mg cholesterol | 1,020mg sodium.

Chicken Curry

Serve curry over rice with an array of condiments—the more, the merrier. Chopped cilantro, chopped peanuts, shredded coconut, golden raisins, cucumber sticks, mango chutney, toasted slivered almonds, and plain yogurt are the most popular items but by no means the only possibilities.

PREP 15 minutes plus cooling   **COOK** 1 hour 15 minutes
MAKES 6 main-dish servings.

1 chicken (3½ pounds), cut into 8 pieces

4 medium onions, finely chopped

2 carrots, peeled and finely chopped

2 stalks celery with leaves, finely chopped

8 parsley sprigs

1 lime

4 tablespoons butter or margarine

2 Granny Smith apples, peeled, cored, and chopped

3 garlic cloves, finely chopped

1 tablespoon curry powder

3 tablespoons all-purpose flour

½ cup half-and-half or light cream

⅓ cup golden raisins

2 tablespoons mango chutney, chopped

2 teaspoons minced, peeled fresh ginger

½ teaspoon salt

pinch ground red pepper (cayenne)

1. In 5-quart Dutch oven, combine chicken, one-fourth onions, carrots, celery, and parsley sprigs with just enough *water* to cover. Heat to boiling over high heat. Reduce heat; partially cover and simmer, turning once, until chicken loses its pink color throughout, 25 to 30 minutes. With slotted spoon, transfer chicken to bowl. When cool enough to handle, remove and discard skin and bones; with hands, shred chicken.

2. Meanwhile, strain broth through sieve, discarding vegetables. Return broth to Dutch oven; heat to boiling and boil until reduced to 2 cups. Skim and discard fat from broth; reserve broth.

3. From lime, grate ½ teaspoon peel and squeeze 5 teaspoons juice; reserve.

4. In 12-inch skillet, melt butter over medium heat. Add remaining three-fourths onions, apples, garlic, and curry powder and cook, stirring, until apples are tender, about 10 minutes. Sprinkle with flour, stirring to blend. Gradually add 2 cups reserved broth, stirring constantly until broth has thickened and boils. Stir in reserved lime peel and juice, half-and-half, raisins, chutney, ginger, salt, and ground red pepper. Reduce heat and simmer, stirring occasionally, 5 minutes. Add chicken and heat through.

EACH SERVING About 379 calories | 30g protein | 33g carbohydrate | 14g total fat (7g saturated) | 117mg cholesterol | 449mg sodium.

Cutting Up a Raw Chicken

To remove a leg, cut down between the thigh and the body. Bend the leg portion back; twist to crack the hip joint. Cut through the joint. Repeat for the other leg.

To separate the leg from the thigh, place the leg skin side down and cut through the center joint. Repeat with the other leg.

To remove a wing, pull the wing away from the body, then cut between the wing joint and the breast. Repeat with the other wing.

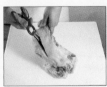

Using kitchen shears, cut through the rib cage along one side of the backbone from the tail to the neck. Repeat on the other side to remove the backbone in one piece.

Place the breast skin side down and cut in half by placing a heavy knife lengthwise along the center of the breastbone. Press the knife down to cut through the bone and meat.

Country Captain Casserole

According to some sources, this dish came to Georgia via India, and the word *captain* is a corruption of *capon*. The predominance of Indian spices seems to support this claim.

PREP 30 minutes **BAKE** I hour **MAKES** 8 main-dish servings.

2 tablespoons plus I teaspoon vegetable oil

2 chickens (3½ pounds each), each cut into 8 pieces and skin removed from all but wings

2 medium onions, chopped

I large Granny Smith apple, peeled, cored, and chopped

I large green pepper, chopped

3 large garlic cloves, finely chopped

I tablespoon grated, peeled fresh ginger

3 tablespoons curry powder

½ teaspoon coarsely ground black pepper

¼ teaspoon ground cumin

I can (28 ounces) plum tomatoes in puree

1¾ cups chicken broth

½ cup dark seedless raisins

I teaspoon salt

¼ cup chopped fresh parsley

1. In nonreactive 8-quart Dutch oven, heat 2 tablespoons oil over medium-high heat until very hot. Add chicken, in batches, and cook until golden brown, about 5 minutes per side. With slotted spoon, transfer chicken pieces to bowl as they are browned.

2. Preheat oven to 350°F. In same Dutch oven, heat remaining 1 teaspoon oil over medium-high heat. Add onions, apple, green pepper, garlic, and ginger; cook, stirring frequently, 2 minutes. Reduce heat to medium; cover and cook 5 minutes longer.

3. Stir in curry powder, black pepper, and cumin; cook 1 minute. Add tomatoes with their puree, broth, raisins, salt, and chicken pieces. Heat to boiling over high heat; boil 1 minute. Cover and place in oven. Bake 1 hour. To serve, sprinkle with parsley.

EACH SERVING About 347 calories | 43g protein | 19g carbohydrate | 11g total fat (2g saturated) | 133mg cholesterol | 825mg sodium.

Chicken Mole

Mole (MO-lay) is a thick, rich, dark brown Mexican sauce traditionally made with dried chiles, spices, seeds such as pumpkin, nuts, and a small amount of unsweetened chocolate. Chicken Mole should be served over rice to soak up the spicy mole and with crisp tortillas.

PREP 10 minutes **COOK** 45 minutes **MAKES** 6 main-dish servings.

I can (14½ ounces) diced tomatoes

I can (4 to 4½ ounces) chopped mild green chiles

½ cup whole blanched almonds

½ small onion, coarsely chopped

I small garlic clove, peeled

I tablespoon chili powder

I teaspoon ground cumin

I teaspoon ground coriander

¾ teaspoon ground cinnamon

¾ teaspoon salt

½ teaspoon sugar

I tablespoon olive oil

3 pounds bone-in chicken parts, skin removed from all but wings

½ square (½ ounce) unsweetened chocolate, chopped

¼ cup water

2 tablespoons chopped fresh cilantro

1. Prepare mole sauce: In blender or in food processor with knife blade attached, puree tomatoes, chiles, almonds, onion, garlic, chili powder, cumin, coriander, cinnamon, salt, and sugar until smooth.

2. In nonstick 12-inch skillet, heat oil over medium-high heat until very hot. Add chicken and cook until golden brown, about 5 minutes per side. With slotted spoon, transfer chicken pieces to large bowl as they are browned.

3. Add mole sauce, chocolate, and water to skillet; cook, stirring, until chocolate melts. Return chicken to skillet; heat to boiling. Reduce heat; cover and simmer until chicken loses its pink color throughout, 30 to 35 minutes. To serve, sprinkle with cilantro.

EACH SERVING About 263 calories | 27g protein | 9g carbohydrate | 14g total fat (3g saturated) | 76mg cholesterol | 617mg sodium.

Chicken, Osso-Buco Style

Classic Italian osso buco is made with veal shanks braised in a flavorful tomato sauce. In our version, we made the same kind of sauce but substituted skinless chicken thighs for the veal shanks, so the dish is lighter and more affordable.

PREP 10 minutes   **COOK** 40 minutes   **MAKES** 4 main-dish servings.

2 tablespoons vegetable oil

8 large chicken thighs (2½ pounds), skin and fat removed

½ teaspoon salt

8 ounces carrots, peeled and finely chopped

1 large onion, diced

1 large stalk celery, finely chopped

1 can (14½ to 16 ounces) stewed tomatoes

chopped parsley

grated lemon peel

1. In 12-inch skillet, heat oil over medium-high heat until very hot. Add chicken thighs and salt and cook until chicken is golden on all sides. With slotted spoon, transfer chicken to bowl.

2. Add carrots, onion, and celery to skillet and cook until lightly browned. Return chicken to skillet. Stir in stewed tomatoes; heat to boiling over high heat. Reduce heat to low; cover and simmer until chicken loses its pink color throughout, about 25 minutes. Sprinkle with chopped parsley and grated lemon peel.

EACH SERVING About 330 calories | 34g protein | 18g carbohydrate | 14g total fat (3g saturated) | 135mg cholesterol | 700mg sodium.

Moroccan-Style Tagine

In Morocco, savory stews called *tagines* are traditionally cooked in special vessels, also called *tagines*. While these stews can be made in any casserole or Dutch oven, the tagine cooker, with its conical top, promotes steaming and self-basting for very juicy, tender results, and provides a dramatic presentation of the stew.

PREP 20 minutes   **COOK** 1 hour   **MAKES** 6 main-dish servings.

2 tablespoons olive oil

6 large chicken thighs (2 pounds), skin and fat removed

1/2 teaspoon salt

1/2 teaspoon ground black pepper

1 large lemon

1 pound carrots, cut into 3/4-inch pieces

1 jumbo onion (1 pound), chopped

3 garlic cloves, coarsely chopped

1 cinnamon stick (3 inches)

2 teaspoons ground coriander

2 teaspoons ground cumin

1/4 teaspoon turmeric

1 can (15 to 19 ounces) garbanzo beans, rinsed and drained

1 3/4 cups chicken broth

1/3 cup dark raisins

1/3 cup pitted green olives, quartered

1 box (10 ounces) plain couscous

1/2 cup loosely packed fresh cilantro leaves, coarsely chopped

1. In 6-quart Dutch oven, heat oil over medium-high heat; add chicken and sprinkle with salt and pepper. Cook until browned on both sides, 8 to 10 minutes.

2. Meanwhile, from lemon, cut peel and white pith. Holding lemon over 1-cup liquid measuring cup to catch juice, cut on either side of membranes to release each section, allowing fruit and juice to drop into cup. Squeeze membranes to release any excess juice. You should have 1/4 cup lemon juice and sections.

3. Transfer chicken to plate. To drippings in Dutch oven, add carrots, onion, garlic, and cinnamon; cook, stirring occasionally, until onion is golden brown, about 10 minutes. Add coriander, cumin, and turmeric, and cook, stirring, 1 minute.

4. Add beans, broth, raisins, olives, lemon segments and juice, and chicken with its juices to Dutch oven; heat to boiling over high heat. Reduce

heat to medium-low; cover and simmer until chicken loses its pink color throughout, about 25 minutes.

5. Meanwhile, prepare couscous as label directs.

6. To serve, fluff couscous with fork. Stir cilantro into chicken mixture. Spoon chicken thighs with sauce over couscous.

EACH SERVING About 540 calories | 35g protein | 71g carbohydrate | 13g total fat (2g saturated) | 94mg cholesterol | 940mg sodium.

Is It Safe to Eat?

Sometimes, although the juices run clear and the chicken has reached the proper temperature for doneness, the meat may retain a bit of pink color. In properly cooked chicken, the pink color is caused by hemoglobin (an iron-containing compound found in red blood cells). It's usually most noticeable in young chickens, which have less fat than mature ones. This color will remain no matter how long you cook the meat, but it is safe to eat. In some other cases, the meat near the bone is a dark color. This is a natural condition that occurs primarily in young broiler-fryers. Because their porous bones are not completely calcified, they allow seepage of pigment from the marrow to the bone's surface. The pigment may adhere to surrounding meat and turn darker during slow freezing (as in most home freezers), then cooking. If you find it unappealing, simply cut it away—although it is safe to eat.

Ragoût of Chicken, White Beans, and Tomatoes

A ragoût is a thick stew made with or without vegetables. We've included celery, carrots, and beans for a hearty one-pot meal.

PREP 15 minutes **COOK** 45 minutes **MAKES** 6 main-dish servings.

2 tablespoons vegetable oil

6 large chicken thighs (2$^{1}/_{2}$ pounds), skin and fat removed

$^{3}/_{4}$ teaspoon salt

3 medium stalks celery, cut into 1-inch-thick slices

3 medium carrots, peeled and cut into $^{1}/_{4}$-inch-thick slices

1 large onion, chopped

$^{1}/_{4}$ teaspoon coarsely ground black pepper

1 garlic clove, crushed with garlic press or finely minced

1 can (14$^{1}/_{2}$ to 16 ounces) stewed tomatoes

2 cans (16 ounces each) Great Northern beans, rinsed and drained

$^{1}/_{4}$ cup chopped fresh basil leaves or 1$^{1}/_{2}$ teaspoons dried basil

1. In 8-quart Dutch oven, heat oil over medium-high heat until very hot. Add chicken thighs and $^{1}/_{4}$ teaspoon salt and cook until chicken is golden brown on all sides. With slotted spoon, transfer chicken thighs to plate.

2. Add celery, carrots, onion, pepper, and remaining $^{1}/_{2}$ teaspoon salt to Dutch oven and cook, stirring occasionally, until vegetables are tender-crisp and golden brown. Stir in garlic; cook, stirring, 1 minute.

3. Add stewed tomatoes, breaking them up with side of spoon. Return chicken thighs to Dutch oven; heat to boiling over high heat. Reduce heat to medium-low; cover and simmer until chicken loses its pink color throughout, about 25 minutes.

4. Transfer chicken thighs to warm platter. Stir beans and basil into Dutch oven; heat through. To serve, spoon bean and tomato mixture around chicken thighs on platter.

EACH SERVING About 310 calories | 29g protein | 27g carbohydrate | 10g total fat (2g saturated) | 90mg cholesterol | 820mg sodium.

Arroz con Pollo

From San Juan to Miami to Madrid, different versions of this comforting chicken-and-rice dish are served almost anywhere Spanish is spoken.

PREP 15 minutes   **COOK** 40 minutes   **MAKES** 4 main-dish servings.

I tablespoon vegetable oil

6 medium chicken thighs (1½ pounds), skin and fat removed

I medium onion, finely chopped

I red pepper, chopped

I garlic clove, finely chopped

⅛ teaspoon ground red pepper (cayenne)

I cup regular long-grain rice

1¾ cups chicken broth

¼ cup water

I strip (3" by ½") lemon peel

¼ teaspoon dried oregano

¼ teaspoon salt

I cup frozen peas

¼ cup chopped pimiento-stuffed olives (salad olives)

¼ cup chopped fresh cilantro

lemon wedges

1. In 5-quart Dutch oven, heat oil over medium-high heat until very hot. Add chicken and cook until golden brown, about 5 minutes per side. With slotted spoon, transfer chicken pieces to bowl as they are browned.

2. Reduce heat to medium. Add onion and red pepper to Dutch oven and cook until tender, about 5 minutes. Stir in garlic and ground red pepper and cook 30 seconds. Add rice and cook, stirring, 1 minute. Stir in broth, water, lemon peel, oregano, salt, and chicken; heat to boiling. Reduce heat; cover and simmer until chicken loses its pink color throughout, about 20 minutes.

3. Stir in peas; cover and heat through. Remove from heat and let stand 5 minutes.

4. Transfer chicken to serving bowl. Sprinkle with olives and cilantro; serve with lemon wedges.

EACH SERVING About 387 calories | 26g protein | 48g carbohydrate | 9g total fat (2g saturated) | 81mg cholesterol | 927mg sodium.

Chicken Bouillabaisse

Serve in oversized soup bowls with a dollop of aïoli (garlic mayonnaise) and thickly sliced French bread toasts.

PREP 1 hour BAKE 30 minutes MAKES 4 main-dish servings.

1 tablespoon olive oil

8 large chicken thighs (2½ pounds), skin and fat removed

2 large carrots, peeled and finely chopped

1 medium onion, finely chopped

1 large fennel bulb (1½ pounds), cut into ¼-inch-thick slices

½ cup water

3 garlic cloves, finely chopped

1 can (14½ ounces) diced tomatoes

1¾ cups chicken broth

½ cup dry white wine

2 tablespoons anisette (anise-flavored liqueur; optional)

¼ teaspoon dried thyme

¼ teaspoon salt

⅛ teaspoon ground red pepper (cayenne)

1 bay leaf

pinch saffron threads

1. In 5-quart Dutch oven, heat oil over medium-high heat until very hot. Add chicken, in batches, and cook until golden brown, about 5 minutes per side. With slotted spoon, transfer chicken to bowl as it is browned.

2. Add carrots and onion to Dutch oven and cook over medium heat, stirring occasionally, until tender and golden, about 10 minutes. Transfer to bowl with chicken.

3. Preheat oven to 350°F. Add fennel and water to Dutch oven, stirring to loosen browned bits from bottom of pot. Cook over medium heat, stirring occasionally, until fennel is tender and browned, about 7 minutes. Add garlic and cook 3 minutes.

4. Return chicken and carrot mixture to Dutch oven. Add tomatoes with their juice, broth, wine, anisette, if using, thyme, salt, ground red pepper, bay leaf, and saffron; heat to boiling. Cover and place in oven. Bake until chicken loses its pink color throughout, about 30 minutes. Discard bay leaf.

EACH SERVING About 317 calories | 36g protein | 18g carbohydrate | 11g total fat (2g saturated) | 135mg cholesterol | 1,036mg sodium.

Easy Aïoli

Aïoli (ay-OH-lee) is a very garlicky mayonnaise from Provence. Our recipe reduces the garlic's harshness by cooking it. Wonderful as a dip for vegetables or seafood, it is also the traditional condiment for Bouillabaisse.

In 2-quart saucepan combine **4 cups water** and **1 teaspoon salt**; heat to boiling. Add **14 cloves of unpeeled garlic** (1 head) and boil until garlic has softened, about 20 minutes. Drain. When cool enough to handle, squeeze soft garlic from each clove into a small bowl. In blender, puree garlic, **1/2 cup mayonnaise, 2 teaspoons fresh lemon juice**, **1/2 teaspoon Dijon mustard**, **1/8 teaspoon salt**, and **1/8 teaspoon ground red pepper (cayenne)** until smooth. With blender running, through hole in cover, add **1/4 cup extravirgin olive oil** in slow, steady stream until mixture is thickened and creamy. Transfer to small bowl; cover and refrigerate up to 4 hours. Makes about 1/4 cup.

Creole Chicken Gumbo

Gumbo gets much of its rich flavor from a deeply browned roux made with a generous amount of fat. Here, the flour is browned in the oven, which results in the same flavor and color without the fat. This makes a big batch—leftovers can be frozen.

PREP 1 hour 10 minutes plus cooling **COOK** 1 hour 30 minutes
MAKES 18 cups, or 12 main-dish servings.

²⁄₃ cup all-purpose flour

12 large chicken thighs (3¹⁄₂ pounds), fat removed

12 ounces fully cooked andouille or kielbasa sausage, cut into ¹⁄₂-inch-thick slices

6 cups chicken broth

1 can (6 ounces) tomato paste

2 cups water

2 medium onions, thinly sliced

12 ounces okra, sliced, or 1 package (10 ounces) frozen cut okra, thawed

1 large yellow pepper, chopped

4 stalks celery with leaves, cut into ¹⁄₄-inch-thick slices

³⁄₄ cup chopped fresh parsley

4 garlic cloves, thinly sliced

2 bay leaves

1¹⁄₂ teaspoons salt

1 teaspoon dried thyme

1 teaspoon ground red pepper (cayenne)

1 teaspoon ground black pepper

¹⁄₂ teaspoon ground allspice

1 can (14 to 16 ounces) tomatoes, drained and chopped

¹⁄₂ cup finely chopped green-onion tops

2 tablespoons distilled white vinegar

3 cups regular long-grain rice, cooked as label directs

1. Preheat oven to 375°F. Place flour in oven-safe 12-inch skillet (if skillet is not oven-safe, wrap handle with double layer of foil). Bake until flour begins to brown, about 25 minutes. Stir with wooden spoon, breaking up any lumps. Bake, stirring flour every 10 minutes, until it turns nut brown, about 35 minutes longer. Remove flour from oven and let cool. Strain flour through sieve to remove any lumps.

2. Heat nonreactive 8-quart Dutch oven over medium-high heat until very hot. Cook chicken, skin side down first, in batches, until golden brown, about 5 minutes per side. Transfer chicken pieces to large bowl as they are browned. Add sausage to Dutch oven and cook over medium

heat, stirring constantly, until lightly browned, about 5 minutes. With slotted spoon, transfer sausage to bowl with chicken.

3. Reduce heat to medium-low. Gradually stir in browned flour, about 3 tablespoons at a time, and cook, stirring constantly, 2 minutes.

4. Immediately add broth, stirring until browned bits are loosened from bottom of pan. Blend tomato paste with water and add to Dutch oven. Stir in onions, okra, yellow pepper, celery, $\frac{1}{4}$ cup parsley, garlic, bay leaves, salt, thyme, ground red pepper, black pepper, and allspice. Add sausage, chicken, and tomatoes. Heat to boiling over high heat. Reduce heat and simmer until liquid has thickened, about 1 hour.

5. Add remaining $\frac{1}{2}$ cup parsley, green onions, and vinegar; heat through. Remove from heat; cover and let stand 10 minutes. Discard bay leaves. Serve gumbo in bowls over rice.

EACH SERVING About 447 calories | 27g protein | 28g carbohydrate | 25g total fat (8g saturated) | 107mg cholesterol | 1,357mg sodium.

Hearty Chicken and Vegetable Stew

Touches of tarragon, wine, and cream transform this family dish into luscious company fare. Use an 8-quart Dutch oven if you want to double the recipe.

PREP 45 minutes **COOK** 1 hour **MAKES** 4 main-dish servings.

2 tablespoons olive oil

2 tablespoons butter or margarine

1 pound skinless, boneless chicken breast halves, cut into 1 1/2-inch pieces

1/2 pound mushrooms, trimmed and thickly sliced

3 medium carrots (8 ounces), peeled and cut into 1-inch pieces

2 medium leeks (4 ounces each), cut into 3/4-inch pieces

1 fennel bulb (1 pound), trimmed and cut into thin wedges

3/4 pound red potatoes, cut into 1-inch pieces

1 bay leaf

1/4 teaspoon dried tarragon

1/2 cup dry white wine

1 3/4 cups chicken broth

1/4 cup water

1 cup half-and-half or light cream

3 tablespoons all-purpose flour

1 cup frozen peas, thawed

3/4 teaspoon salt

1. In 5-quart Dutch oven, heat 1 tablespoon olive oil over medium-high heat until hot. Add 1 tablespoon butter; melt. Add chicken and cook until chicken is golden and just loses its pink color throughout. With slotted spoon, transfer chicken to medium bowl.

2. Add mushrooms to Dutch oven and cook until golden (do not over-brown). Transfer mushrooms to bowl with chicken.

3. Add remaining 1 tablespoon olive oil to Dutch oven and heat until hot. Add remaining 1 tablespoon butter; heat until melted. Add carrots, leeks, fennel, potatoes, bay leaf, and tarragon. Cook vegetables, stirring occasionally, until fennel is translucent and leeks are wilted, 10 to 15 minutes.

4. Add wine; cook, stirring, 2 minutes. Add chicken broth and water; heat to boiling over high heat. Reduce heat to low; cover and simmer until vegetables are tender, about 20 minutes.

5. In cup, mix half-and-half and flour until smooth. Stir half-and-half mixture into vegetable mixture; heat to boiling over high heat. Reduce heat to medium; cook 1 minute to thicken slightly. Stir in chicken, mushrooms, peas, and salt; heat through. Discard bay leaf.

EACH SERVING About 550 calories | 36g protein | 47g carbohydrate | 22g total fat (10g saturated) | 104mg cholesterol | 1,202mg sodium.

Chicken Thighs Provençal

The combination of thyme, basil, fennel, and orange is quintessentially Provençal and makes sensational chicken.

PREP 30 minutes **COOK** 1 hour 15 minutes **MAKES** 8 main-dish servings.

2 pounds skinless, boneless chicken thighs, cut into quarters and fat removed

¾ teaspoon salt

3 teaspoons olive oil

2 red peppers, cut into ¼-inch-wide strips

1 yellow pepper, cut into ¼-inch-wide strips

1 jumbo onion (1 pound), thinly sliced

3 garlic cloves, crushed with garlic press

1 can (28 ounces) plum tomatoes

¼ teaspoon dried thyme

¼ teaspoon fennel seeds, crushed

3 strips (3" by 1" each) orange peel

½ cup loosely packed fresh basil leaves, chopped

1. Sprinkle chicken with ½ teaspoon salt. In nonreactive 5-quart Dutch oven, heat 1 teaspoon oil over medium-high heat until very hot. Add half of chicken and cook until golden brown, about 5 minutes per side. With slotted spoon, transfer chicken pieces to bowl as they are browned. Repeat with 1 teaspoon oil and remaining chicken.

2. Reduce heat to medium. To drippings in Dutch oven, add remaining 1 teaspoon oil. Add red and yellow peppers, onion, and remaining ¼ teaspoon salt, and cook, stirring frequently, until vegetables are tender and lightly browned, about 20 minutes. Add garlic; cook 1 minute longer.

3. Return chicken to Dutch oven. Add tomatoes with their juice, thyme, fennel seeds, and orange peel; heat to boiling, breaking up tomatoes with side of spoon. Reduce heat; cover and simmer until chicken loses its pink color throughout, about 15 minutes.

4. Transfer to serving bowl and sprinkle with basil to serve.

EACH SERVING About 204 calories | 24g protein | 12g carbohydrate | 7g total fat (1g saturated) | 94mg cholesterol | 480mg sodium.

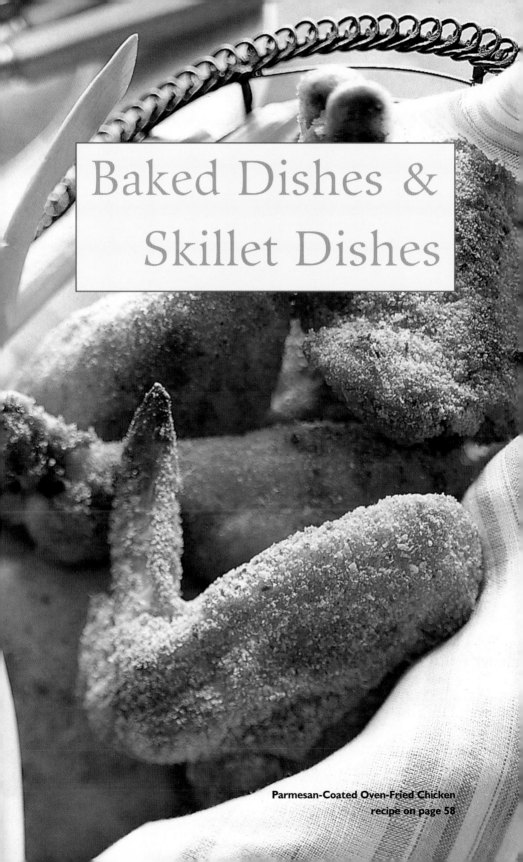

Baked Dishes & Skillet Dishes

Parmesan-Coated Oven-Fried Chicken
recipe on page 58

Parmesan-Coated Oven-Fried Chicken

Coat chicken pieces with a spicy cornmeal and bread-crumb mixture, then lightly spray with cooking spray and "fry" on a cookie sheet in the oven. This technique cuts down on fat calories and cleanup—what could be better!

PREP 15 minutes **BAKE** 35 minutes **MAKES** 4 main-dish servings.

olive-oil nonstick cooking spray

$^1/_2$ cup plain dried bread crumbs

$^1/_4$ cup grated Parmesan cheese

2 tablespoons yellow cornmeal

$^1/_2$ teaspoon ground red pepper (cayenne)

1 egg white

$^1/_2$ teaspoon salt

1 chicken (about 3 $^1/_2$ pounds), cut into 8 pieces and skin removed

1. Preheat oven to 425°F. Spray 15$^1/_2$" by 10$^1/_2$" jelly-roll pan with cooking spray.

2. On waxed paper, mix bread crumbs, Parmesan, cornmeal, and ground red pepper. In pie plate, beat egg white and salt.

3. Dip each piece of chicken in egg-white mixture, then coat with bread-crumb mixture. Place chicken in prepared pan; spray lightly with cooking spray. Bake chicken until coating is crisp and juices run clear when thickest part is pierced with tip of knife, about 35 minutes.

EACH SERVING About 325 calories | 6g protein | 14g carbohydrate | 8g total fat (3g saturated) | 137mg cholesterol | 660mg sodium.

Classic Fried Chicken

Here it is—our favorite recipe for this all-time classic.

PREP 35 minutes plus chilling and standing **COOK** 1¼ hours
MAKES 8 main-dish servings.

2 cups buttermilk

2 tablespoons hot pepper sauce

1 tablespoon salt

2 chickens (3½ pounds each), each
  cut into 8 pieces

2 cups all-purpose flour

1½ teaspoons baking powder

1 teaspoon ground black pepper

1 teaspoon paprika

5 cups vegetable oil or shortening

1. In 2-gallon ziptight bag, combine buttermilk, hot pepper sauce, and 1 teaspoon salt. Add chicken, turning to coat. Seal bag and place in a bowl. Refrigerate chicken 2 hours to marinate, turning bag over once.

2. In large bowl, stir flour, baking powder, pepper, paprika, and remaining 2 teaspoons salt until well mixed. Remove chicken, a few pieces at a time, from marinade, shaking off excess. Add chicken to flour mixture, turning to coat well. Place on wire rack, set over waxed paper, without touching. Repeat with remaining chicken; let stand 15 minutes to set coating.

3. Meanwhile, preheat oven to 250°F. Line two 15½" by 10½" jelly-roll pans with paper towels. Divide oil between two 12-inch skillets, preferably electric (there should be about ½ inch oil in each skillet), and heat over medium heat until temperature reaches 360°F on deep-fry thermometer.

4. To each skillet, add 4 pieces chicken, skin side down, being careful not to crowd pieces. Cover skillets and cook until chicken is light golden brown on bottom, 4 to 5 minutes. Turn pieces over and cook, covered, reducing heat to medium-low if necessary to maintain temperature of 300°F, 8 to 10 minutes longer for white meat, 13 to 15 minutes longer for dark meat, turning pieces every 4 to 5 minutes, or until well browned on all sides, and juices run clear when thickest part is pierced with the tip of knife.

5. Transfer chicken to lined jelly-roll pans to drain. Keep warm in oven. Repeat with remaining chicken.

EACH SERVING About 655 calories | 50g protein | 11g carbohydrate |
45g total fat (9g saturated) | 155mg cholesterol | 622mg sodium.

Rosemary-Apricot Chicken

A crowd pleaser to serve up hot or cold, this dish is perfect for a picnic or potluck supper offering. If you'll have access to a grill for your picnic, bake the marinated chicken at home without the glaze, then reheat it on the grill, brushing with the apricot mixture just before removing it from the heat.

PREP 20 minutes plus marinating **BAKE** 45 minutes **MAKES** 12 main-dish servings.

2 teaspoons salt

1 teaspoon dried rosemary, crumbled

$^{1}/_{2}$ teaspoon coarsely ground black pepper

4 garlic cloves, crushed with garlic press

3 chickens (3 pounds each), each cut into quarters, skin removed

$^{1}/_{2}$ cup apricot jam

2 tablespoons fresh lemon juice

2 teaspoons Dijon mustard

1. In cup, mix salt, rosemary, pepper, and garlic. Rub rosemary mixture over chicken quarters; cover and refrigerate in large bowl about 2 hours.

2. Preheat oven to 350°F. Place chicken quarters, skinned side up, in 2 large roasting pans (17" by 11$^{1}/_{2}$" each) or 2 jelly-roll pans (15$^{1}/_{2}$" by 10$^{1}/_{2}$" each). Bake chicken 25 minutes on 2 oven racks, rotating pans between upper and lower racks halfway through baking.

3. Meanwhile, in small bowl, with fork, mix apricot jam, lemon juice, and mustard. Brush apricot mixture over chicken; bake, rotating pans after 10 minutes until juices run clear when thickest part of chicken is pierced with tip of knife, about 20 minutes longer. Serve chicken hot, or cover and refrigerate to serve cold later.

EACH SERVING About 230 calories | 35g protein | 9g carbohydrate | 5g total fat (1g saturated) | 114mg cholesterol | 540mg sodium.

Carolina Chicken Pilau

This simple recipe, made with bacon, onion, and chicken, is based on an old-fashioned southern rice dish. For best flavor, cook the chicken breasts on the bone. If you have time, remove the chicken from the bone, shred the meat, and return it to the rice mixture; toss before serving.

PREP 20 minutes   **COOK** about 45 minutes   **MAKES** 4 main-dish servings.

1 teaspoon olive oil

4 small bone-in chicken breast halves (about 2³/₄ pounds), skin removed

2 slices bacon, cut into ¹/₄-inch pieces

1 large onion (12 ounces), cut lengthwise in half, then thinly sliced crosswise

1 cup long-grain white rice

1³/₄ cups chicken broth

¹/₂ cup water

¹/₄ teaspoon salt

¹/₄ teaspoon coarsely ground black pepper

¹/₂ cup loosely packed fresh parsley leaves, chopped

1. In nonstick 12-inch skillet, heat oil over medium-high heat until hot. Add chicken and cook, turning once, until golden, about 8 minutes. Transfer chicken to plate.

2. Reduce heat to medium; add bacon and cook, stirring frequently, until browned, about 4 minutes. With slotted spoon, transfer bacon to small bowl. Discard all but 2 teaspoons drippings from skillet.

3. Add onion to same skillet and cook, covered, stirring occasionally, until tender and lightly browned, about 10 minutes. Add rice and stir until evenly coated. Stir in bacon, broth, water, salt, and pepper. Return chicken to skillet; heat to boiling over medium-high heat. Reduce heat to medium-low and cook, covered, until juices run clear when thickest part of breast is pierced with tip of knife and rice is tender, 20 to 25 minutes. Sprinkle with parsley to serve.

EACH SERVING About 390 calories | 36g protein | 41g carbohydrate | 8g total fat (2g saturated) | 81mg cholesterol | 725mg sodium.

Panko-Mustard Chicken

If you have an Asian market nearby, opt for the panko crumbs; coarser than regular bread crumbs, they produce an extra crunchy crust.

PREP 15 minutes **BAKE** 12 minutes **MAKES** 4 main-dish servings.

1 medium shallot, minced

2 tablespoons butter or margarine

2 tablespoons Dijon mustard
  with seeds

2 teaspoons chopped fresh tarragon

$^1/_2$ cup panko (Japanese-style
  bread crumbs) or plain dried
  bread crumbs

4 medium skinless, boneless chicken
  breast halves (1$^1/_4$ pounds)

$^1/_4$ teaspoon salt

1. Preheat oven to 475°F.

2. In small microwave-safe bowl, place shallot and 2 teaspoons butter. Microwave on High 1 minute. Stir in mustard and tarragon.

3. In another small microwave-safe bowl, place remaining butter. Microwave on High until melted, 15 to 20 seconds. Stir in panko until mixed.

4. Arrange chicken breasts in 15$^1/_2$" by 10$^1/_2$" jelly-roll pan; sprinkle with salt. Spread mustard mixture evenly over breasts. Top with panko mixture, patting gently to adhere. Bake in top third of oven until chicken loses its pink color throughout, 12 to 15 minutes.

EACH SERVING About 270 calories | **35g protein** | **7g carbohydrate** |
10g total fat (5g saturated) | **107mg cholesterol** | **347mg sodium.**

Chicken Breasts Stuffed with Sun-Dried Tomatoes and Basil

When you have used up all the sun-dried tomatoes in the jar, don't discard any leftover oil; you can use it to cook with or to make salad dressing.

PREP 15 minutes **BAKE** 40 minutes **MAKES** 4 main-dish servings.

^{1}/4 cup oil-packed sun-dried tomatoes with 1 tablespoon oil from tomatoes

^{1}/4 cup chopped fresh basil leaves

2 tablespoons grated Parmesan cheese

1 teaspoon coarsely ground black pepper

4 medium bone-in chicken breast halves (2 pounds)

^{1}/2 teaspoon salt

1. Preheat oven to 425°F. Coarsely chop sun-dried tomatoes. In small bowl, mix chopped basil, sun-dried tomatoes, Parmesan, and ^{1}/2 teaspoon pepper.

2. Carefully push fingers between skin and meat of each chicken breast to form a pocket; stuff equal amounts of basil mixture into each pocket. Place chicken breasts, skin side up, in 13" by 9" glass baking dish; brush with oil from sun-dried tomatoes and sprinkle with salt and remaining ^{1}/2 teaspoon pepper.

3. Bake chicken, basting occasionally with pan drippings, until juices run clear when thickest part of chicken is pierced with tip of knife, 35 to 40 minutes.

EACH SERVING About 320 calories | 39g protein | 5g carbohydrate | 16g total fat (4g saturated) | 105mg cholesterol | 485mg sodium.

Smoky Almond Chicken

Pairing barbecue sauce with the almond–bread crumb coating enhances the smoky flavor of the almonds. Serve with oven-roasted vegetables, which can cook at the same time as the chicken.

PREP 10 minutes   **BAKE** 15 minutes   **MAKES** 4 main-dish servings.

$^1/_2$ cup salted smoked almonds

1 slice firm white bread, torn into pieces

$^1/_4$ teaspoon ground black pepper

$^1/_4$ cup reduced-fat sour cream

$^1/_2$ cup bottled barbecue sauce

4 small skinless, boneless chicken breast halves (1 pound)

1. Preheat oven to 400°F. In food processor with knife blade attached, pulse almonds, bread, and pepper until coarsely chopped; transfer to waxed paper. In pie plate, mix sour cream with 1 tablespoon barbecue sauce.

2. Dip chicken into sour-cream mixture, then coat with almond mixture, pressing firmly so mixture adheres; arrange on cookie sheet.

3. Bake chicken until juices run clear when thickest part of the chicken loses its pink color throughout, 12 to 15 minutes; serve with remaining barbecue sauce.

EACH SERVING About 330 calories | 32g protein | 11g carbohydrate | 7g total fat (3g saturated) | 78mg cholesterol | 485mg sodium.

Poached Chicken Piccata

Poaching keeps these chicken breasts moist and juicy. The flavorful poaching broth is used as the base for the piquant lemon-and-caper sauce.

PREP 10 minutes **COOK** 12 minutes **MAKES** 4 main-dish servings.

1½ cups water

1 bay leaf

½ teaspoon salt

4 small skinless, boneless chicken
   breast halves (1 pound)

1 lemon, thinly sliced

2 teaspoons cornstarch

3 tablespoons capers, drained

2 teaspoons butter or margarine
   (optional)

1. In 10-inch skillet, heat water to boiling over high heat. Add bay leaf, salt, chicken, and 2 lemon slices; heat to boiling. Reduce heat to low; cover and simmer until chicken loses its pink color throughout, 10 to 12 minutes. With slotted spoon; transfer chicken to platter; keep warm.

2. Drain poaching liquid through coarse sieve set over medium bowl; discard solids. Return poaching liquid to skillet. In cup, blend cornstarch and 1 tablespoon poaching liquid until smooth. With wire whisk, beat cornstarch mixture into poaching liquid until blended; heat to boiling over high heat. Add capers; cook, stirring constantly, 1 minute. Stir in butter, if you like. Pour the caper sauce over chicken and garnish with remaining lemon slices.

EACH SERVING About 130 calories | 26g protein | 2g carbohydrate | 2g total fat (0g saturated) | 66mg cholesterol | 555mg sodium.

Chicken with Smashed Potatoes, Potpie Style

Instead of a regular piecrust, a creamy chicken and vegetable mixture is spooned over potatoes coarsely mashed with their skins for a hearty, less labor-intensive meal.

PREP 10 minutes **COOK** 20 minutes **MAKES** 4 main-dish servings.

1 ½ pounds baby red potatoes, each cut in half

1 tablespoon vegetable oil

4 medium skinless, boneless chicken breast halves (1 ¼ pounds)

½ teaspoon salt

¼ teaspoon ground black pepper

1 ½ cups matchstick carrot strips (half 10-ounce bag)

1 cup chicken broth

¼ cup heavy or whipping cream

½ teaspoon dried tarragon, crumbled

1 cup tiny frozen peas, thawed

1 tablespoon butter or margarine

1. In 5-quart Dutch oven, combine potatoes and enough *water* to cover; heat to boiling over high heat. Reduce heat to low; cover and simmer until potatoes are fork-tender, about 12 minutes.

2. While potatoes are cooking, in nonstick 12-inch skillet, heat oil over medium-high heat until hot. Add chicken and sprinkle with ¼ teaspoon salt and ⅛ teaspoon pepper; cook 6 minutes. Turn chicken. Reduce heat to medium; cover and cook until chicken loses its pink color throughout, 8 minutes longer. Transfer chicken to plate; keep warm.

3. To same skillet, add carrots, broth, cream, and tarragon; cover and cook over medium-high heat until carrots are tender, 5 minutes. Remove skillet from heat and stir in peas.

4. Coarsely mash potatoes with butter and remaining ¼ teaspoon salt and ⅛ teaspoon pepper. Spoon potatoes onto platter; top with chicken and vegetable mixture.

EACH SERVING About 460 calories | 39g protein | 43g carbohydrate | 14g total fat (5g saturated) | 111mg cholesterol | 726 mg sodium.

Chicken and Mushroom Potpie with Herb Phyllo Crust

A timeless classic is updated with a crispy phyllo crust instead of a traditional piecrust.

PREP 15 minutes **COOK/BAKE** 50 minutes **MAKES** 8 main-dish servings.

7 tablespoons butter or margarine

2 pounds skinless, boneless chicken breast halves

3/4 teaspoon salt

8 sheets (about 16" by 12" each) fresh or frozen (thawed) phyllo

parsley leaves

1 medium onion, chopped

1 package (8 ounces) whole white mushrooms, each cut into quarters (or into eighths if large)

1 package (4 ounces) sliced mixed wild mushrooms

1/4 cup dry white wine

1 package (10 ounces) frozen peas

1 tablespoon chopped fresh tarragon leaves

1/4 cup all-purpose flour

1 3/4 cups chicken broth

1 cup whole milk

1/4 teaspoon ground black pepper

1. In nonstick 12-inch skillet, melt 1 tablespoon butter over medium-high heat. Add chicken; sprinkle with 1/4 teaspoon salt. Cook 5 minutes. Reduce heat to medium; turn breasts and cook until chicken loses its pink color throughout, 5 to 7 minutes longer. Transfer to cutting board. Preheat oven to 375°F.

2. Meanwhile, in small microwave-safe bowl, heat 3 tablespoons butter in microwave oven on High, stirring once, until melted, about 30 seconds. Remove phyllo from package; keep covered with plastic wrap to prevent it from drying out. Place 1 phyllo sheet on large cookie sheet; lightly brush with some melted butter. Repeat layering with 6 phyllo sheets and melted butter. Arrange parsley leaves on top of phyllo. Top with remaining phyllo sheet and butter. Cut phyllo stack lengthwise in half, then crosswise into 8 equal rectangles. Bake until deep golden, 10 to 12 minutes. Place cookie sheet on wire rack; set aside.

3. Cut chicken breasts into 3/4-inch chunks. Transfer with any juices to large bowl; keep warm.

4. Add onion to drippings in skillet; cook over medium heat, stirring frequently, 5 minutes. Add all mushrooms and cook until tender, 5 minutes. Add wine; heat to boiling. Boil 1 minute. Stir in frozen peas and tarragon; cook just until peas are heated through. Transfer mixture to bowl with chicken; keep warm.

5. In same skillet, melt remaining 3 tablespoons butter over medium-high heat. With wire whisk, stir in flour and cook, stirring frequently, 2 minutes. Gradually whisk in broth and milk; heat to boiling. Boil until mixture has thickened, about 1 minute. Stir in pepper and remaining $^1/_2$ teaspoon salt.

6. Stir sauce into chicken mixture, then spoon mixture into 8 shallow soup bowls. With wide metal spatula, top each with 1 phyllo rectangle.

EACH SERVING About 360 calories | 33g protein | 23g carbohydrate | 14g total fat (8g saturated) | 97mg cholesterol | 769mg sodium.

Chicken Korma with Scented Rice

The spice-scented rice is the perfect foil for this creamy curried chicken.

PREP 15 minutes **COOK** 30 minutes **MAKES** 6 main-dish servings.

1 tablespoon olive oil

2 whole cloves

2 whole cardamom pods

1 1/2 cinnamon sticks (5 inches)

1 1/2 cups long-grain white rice

1 1/4 teaspoons salt

3 cups water

1/2 cup sliced almonds

2 tablespoons butter or margarine

1 1/4 pounds skinless, boneless chicken breast halves, thinly sliced crosswise

1/4 teaspoon ground cardamom

1/4 teaspoon turmeric

pinch ground cloves

1 large onion (12 ounces), cut in half, then thinly sliced

2 garlic cloves, minced

1 tablespoon chopped, peeled fresh ginger

1 cup heavy or whipping cream

1/2 cup loosely packed fresh cilantro leaves, chopped

1. Prepare rice: In 2-quart saucepan, heat oil over medium heat. Add whole cloves, cardamom pods, and 1/2 cinnamon stick; cook, stirring, 15 seconds. Add rice and cook, stirring to coat with oil, 1 minute,. Add 3/4 teaspoon salt and water; heat to boiling over high heat. Reduce heat to low; cover and simmer until rice is tender, about 15 minutes.

2. Meanwhile, prepare chicken: In nonstick 12-inch skillet over medium-high heat, toast almonds, stirring, 5 minutes; transfer to plate. In same skillet, melt 1 tablespoon butter over medium-high heat. Add half of chicken and cook, stirring constantly, just until chicken loses its pink color throughout, 2 to 3 minutes. With slotted spoon, transfer chicken to bowl. Repeat with remaining chicken.

3. Reduce heat to medium. In same skillet, melt remaining 1 tablespoon butter. Add ground cardamom, turmeric, ground cloves, and remaining cinnamon stick; cook, stirring, just until fragrant, about 30 seconds.

4. Add onion, garlic, and ginger; cover and cook, stirring occasionally, until tender, about 10 minutes. Stir in cream and remaining ½ teaspoon salt; heat to boiling. Boil, uncovered, until mixture has thickened slightly, about 2 minutes.

5. Return chicken with any juices to skillet; heat through. Stir in cilantro and almonds, reserving 2 tablespoons almonds for garnish.

6. Fluff rice with fork. Remove spices from rice. Remove cinnamon stick from chicken.

7. To serve, spoon rice onto 6 dinner plates; top with chicken and sauce. Sprinkle with reserved almonds.

EACH SERVING About 545 calories | 29g protein | 45g carbohydrate | 27g total fat (13g saturated) | 120mg cholesterol | 608mg sodium.

Double-Dipped Potato-Chip Chicken with Quick Slaw

This quick and easy meal is perfect for busy weeknights. If you like, experiment with flavored chips to get a whole new taste experience.

PREP 15 minutes **BAKE** 15 minutes **MAKES** 4 main-dish servings.

4 ounces potato chips (about 4 cups)

1 large egg

4 medium skinless, boneless chicken-breast halves (1 ¼ pounds)

¼ teaspoon plus ⅛ teaspoon ground black pepper

4 cups shredded cabbage mix for coleslaw (about 8 ounces)

1 large carrot, shredded

¼ small red onion, thinly sliced

¼ cup cider vinegar

2 tablespoons vegetable oil

1 teaspoon sugar

½ teaspoon salt

¼ cup light mayonnaise

2 tablespoons barbecue sauce

1. Preheat oven to 450°F.

2. Place potato chips in large self-sealing plastic bag. With rolling pin or bottom of small saucepan, crush chips to make crumbs. (There should be about 1¼ cups crumbs.) With fork, beat egg in pie plate or shallow dish. Dip 1 chicken-breast half in egg, then transfer to crumbs in bag. Press crumbs onto chicken so they adhere. Transfer chicken to ungreased cookie sheet.

3. Repeat with remaining chicken. Dip chicken again in any remaining crumbs in bag so that chicken is completely coated. Return chicken to cookie sheet. Sprinkle both sides of chicken with ¼ teaspoon pepper. Bake 15 minutes or just until chicken loses its pink color throughout.

4. Meanwhile, in large bowl, toss cabbage mix with carrot, onion, vinegar, oil, sugar, salt, and remaining ⅛ teaspoon pepper until well combined.

5. In small bowl, stir mayonnaise and barbecue sauce until blended.

6. To serve, spoon barbecue mayonnaise into 4 small ramekins or custard cups. Place chicken, slaw, and ramekins on 4 dinner plates.

EACH SERVING About 460 calories | 38g protein | 30g carbohydrate | 21g total fat (4g saturated) | 140mg cholesterol | 755mg sodium.

Deviled Chicken Thighs

Skinless chicken thighs are coated with a flavorful mustard mixture and bread crumbs, then baked until crisp and golden. Serve with green beans on the side.

PREP 15 minutes **BAKE** 30 minutes **MAKES** 4 main-dish servings.

$^{1}/_{4}$ **cup creamy mustard (such as Dijonnaise)**

1 **tablespoon Worcestershire sauce**

$^{1}/_{2}$ **cup plain dried bread crumbs**

$^{1}/_{4}$ **cup loosely packed fresh parsley leaves, chopped**

$^{1}/_{2}$ **teaspoon salt**

$^{1}/_{4}$ **teaspoon coarsely ground black pepper**

8 **large chicken thighs (2$^{1}/_{2}$ pounds), skin and fat removed**

1. Preheat oven to 475°F. Lightly grease 15$^{1}/_{2}$" by 10$^{1}/_{2}$" jelly-roll pan. In large bowl, mix creamy mustard and Worcestershire sauce until blended. On waxed paper, combine bread crumbs, parsley, salt, and pepper.

2. Toss chicken thighs with mustard mixture, then roll in crumb mixture until evenly coated; place in jelly-roll pan.

3. Bake thighs 15 minutes; turn thighs and bake until juices run clear when thickest part of thigh is pierced with tip of knife, about 15 minutes longer.

EACH SERVING About 420 calories | 43g protein | 14g carbohydrate | 1g total fat (5g saturated) | 151mg cholesterol | 770mg sodium.

Chicken with Tomatoes and Olives over Polenta

Polenta (cornmeal), a staple in northern Italian kitchens is a welcome change of pace from rice and mashed potatoes.

PREP 15 minutes **COOK** 40 minutes **MAKES** 4 main-dish servings.

CHICKEN

2 tablespoons all-purpose flour

3/4 teaspoon salt

1/4 teaspoon ground black pepper

4 medium chicken leg quarters (2 1/4 pounds), skin and fat removed

1 tablespoon olive oil

1 small onion, cut in half and thinly sliced

1/2 cup dry white wine

1 can (14 1/2 ounces) diced tomatoes

1/2 cup Kalamata olives, pitted and coarsely chopped

4 strips (3" by 1" each) fresh lemon peel

6 sprigs fresh thyme

POLENTA

2 1/4 cups whole milk

1 3/4 cups chicken broth

1 cup yellow cornmeal

2 tablespoons butter or margarine, cut into pieces

1/8 teaspoon ground black pepper

1. Prepare chicken: On waxed paper, combine flour, 1/2 teaspoon salt, and pepper; use to coat chicken legs.

2. In nonstick 12-inch skillet, heat oil over medium heat until hot. Add legs and cook, turning once, until browned, 10 to 12 minutes. Transfer legs to plate.

3. To drippings in skillet, add onion and cook, stirring frequently, until golden brown, about 5 minutes. Add wine; boil until reduced by half, about 2 minutes. Add tomatoes with their juice, olives, lemon peel, thyme sprigs, and remaining 1/4 teaspoon salt. Return legs with any juices to skillet, stirring to coat; heat to boiling over high heat. Reduce heat to low. Cover and simmer until chicken loses its pink color throughout, about 20 minutes.

4. Meanwhile, prepare polenta: In 3-quart saucepan, heat milk and broth to boiling over high heat. Reduce heat to low; gradually whisk in corn-meal. Cook, stirring occasionally, until mixture is very thick, about 10 minutes. Remove saucepan from heat; stir in butter and pepper.

5. Remove lemon peel and thyme sprigs from chicken mixture. Divide polenta among 4 dinner plates; top each with a chicken leg and sauce.

EACH SERVING About 550 calories | 41g protein | 43g carbohydrate | 23g total fat (9g saturated) | 155mg cholesterol | 1,667mg sodium.

Sesame Chicken Thighs with Hoisin Dipping Sauce

A mixture of soybeans, garlic, chile peppers, and spices, hoisin sauce is widely used in Chinese cooking. For this recipe it is used to flavor the chicken as well as a dipping sauce.

PREP 10 minutes **BAKE** 20 minutes **MAKES** 4 main-dish servings.

8 medium chicken thighs (2 pounds), skin and fat removed

1/4 cup plus 2 tablespoons hoisin sauce

2 tablespoons sesame seeds

2 tablespoons chili sauce

1 1/2 teaspoons chopped, peeled fresh ginger

1 1/2 teaspoons rice vinegar

1/4 teaspoon Chinese five-spice powder

1. Preheat oven to 475°F.

2. Arrange chicken thighs in 15 1/2" by 10 1/2" jelly-roll pan. Into cup, pour 1/4 cup hoisin sauce; use to brush both sides of thighs. Sprinkle with sesame seeds. Bake until juices run clear when thickest part of thigh is pierced with knife, 20 to 25 minutes.

3. Meanwhile, prepare dipping sauce: In microwave-safe 1-cup liquid measuring cup, combine chili sauce, ginger, vinegar, five-spice powder, and remaining 2 tablespoons hoisin sauce. Just before serving, heat mixture in microwave oven on High, stirring once, 45 seconds. Serve thighs with dipping sauce.

EACH SERVING About 305 calories | 29g protein | 14g carbohydrate | 14g total fat (4g saturated) | 100mg cholesterol | 535mg sodium.

Bacon-Wrapped Thighs with Chunky Applesauce

You can use a variety of apples for this sauce. For a delicious sweet-tart balance combine Granny Smiths with a sweeter variety, like Golden Delicious.

PREP 15 minutes   **COOK** 20 minutes   **MAKES** 4 main-dish servings.

1 tablespoon balsamic vinegar

1/4 teaspoon salt

8 small skinless, boneless chicken thighs (1 1/2 pounds)

2 pounds apples such as Rome Beauty, McIntosh, or Gala, peeled, cored, and coarsely chopped

1/2 cup apple cider or water

1/4 cup dark raisins

1/4 cup sugar

1/4 teaspoon ground cinnamon

8 slices bacon

1. In medium bowl, with fork, mix vinegar and salt. Add chicken thighs and toss to coat. Set aside.

2. In 3-quart saucepan, combine apples, cider, raisins, sugar, and cinnamon; heat to boiling over high heat. Reduce heat to low; simmer until apples are very tender, about 15 minutes.

3. Meanwhile, wrap 1 slice bacon around each thigh; secure with toothpick. Heat nonstick 12-inch skillet over medium heat until hot. Add thighs and cook, turning once, just until bacon has browned and juices run clear when thickest part of thigh is pierced with knife, 15 to 17 minutes.

4. With potato masher, coarsely mash apples.

5. To serve, discard toothpicks. Spoon applesauce on 4 dinner plates; top each with 2 thighs.

EACH SERVING About 530 calories | 38g protein | 49g carbohydrate | 20g total fat (7g saturated) | 132mg cholesterol | 470mg sodium.

Baked Honey-Lime Drumsticks

We removed the skin from the drumsticks, then baked them with a tangy glaze—perfect finger food for both kids and adults! If you're entertaining a large crowd, prepare the recipe a second time; crowding drumsticks in pans would cause them to steam, so they wouldn't glaze properly.

PREP 20 minutes   **BAKE** 30 minutes   **MAKES** 24 drumsticks.

3 limes, plus wedges for garnish

^{1}/$_4$ cup honey

3 small garlic cloves, crushed with garlic press

1 teaspoon ground coriander

1 teaspoon salt

^{1}/$_2$ teaspoon coarsely ground black pepper

24 medium chicken drumsticks (6 pounds), skin removed

^{1}/$_2$ cup loosely packed fresh parsley or cilantro leaves, chopped

1. Preheat oven to 450°F. From limes, grate 2 teaspoons peel and squeeze ^{1}/$_4$ cup juice.

2. In small bowl, with fork, mix honey, garlic, coriander, salt, pepper, lime juice, and 1 teaspoon lime peel.

3. Arrange chicken on two 15^1/$_2$" by 10^1/$_2$" jelly-roll pans. Drizzle lime mixture over chicken; toss to coat evenly. Place pans on 2 oven racks. Bake drumsticks, rotating pans between upper and lower racks halfway through baking and occasionally brushing chicken with glaze in pan, until juices run clear when thickest part of chicken is pierced with tip of knife, 30 to 35 minutes.

4. Transfer chicken to serving dish. Drizzle with pan juices. Sprinkle with parsley or cilantro and remaining 1 teaspoon lime peel. Serve with lime wedges.

EACH DRUMSTICK About 90 calories | 13g protein | 3g carbohydrate | 3g total fat (1g saturated) | 41mg cholesterol | 130mg sodium.

Sesame Chicken Wings

If you don't have pure maple syrup on hand, you can substitute maple-flavored syrup, honey, or orange marmalade.

PREP 15 minutes   **BAKE** 1 hour   **MAKES** 4 main-dish servings.

3 pounds chicken wings (12 wings)	2 teaspoons Asian sesame oil
3 tablespoons soy sauce	4 tablespoons maple syrup
3 tablespoons dry sherry	1 tablespoon sesame seeds
1 tablespoon grated, peeled fresh ginger	1 small head romaine lettuce, sliced

1. Preheat oven to 400°F. In small roasting pan (13" by 9"), toss chicken wings with soy sauce, sherry, ginger, sesame oil, and 2 tablespoons maple syrup. Bake, basting often with soy-sauce mixture in pan and adding water to pan if mixture looks dry, 45 minutes.

2. After chicken wings have baked 45 minutes, brush with remaining 2 tablespoons maple syrup and sprinkle with sesame seeds. Bake until wings are browned and very tender, about 15 minutes longer.

3. Line platter with lettuce; arrange wings on lettuce. Skim fat from drippings in roasting pan; pour drippings over wings and lettuce.

EACH SERVING About 490 calories | 38g protein | 18g carbohydrate | 29g total fat (8g saturated) | 109mg cholesterol | 890mg sodium.

Spring Meat Loaf with Gremolata Crumbs

Gremolata, a traditional Italian garnish of chopped lemon peel, parsley and garlic, is used to flavor the bread-crumb topping of this vegetable-flecked loaf.

PREP 30 minutes **BAKE** 50 minutes **MAKES** 8 main-dish servings.

4 slices firm white bread

I lemon

2 tablespoons butter or margarine

2 carrots, peeled and cut into
   $^1/_2$-inch chunks

I medium onion, chopped

I medium zucchini (8 ounces),
   cut into $^1/_2$-inch chunks

I$^1/_4$ teaspoons salt

I pound ground chicken meat

2 large eggs, lightly beaten

$^1/_8$ teaspoon ground black pepper

I garlic clove

$^1/_2$ cup loosely packed fresh
   parsley leaves

2 tablespoons extravirgin olive oil

1. Preheat oven to 400°F. While oven preheats, place 2 bread slices on cookie sheet in oven and toast, turning once, until golden, 10 to 15 minutes. Transfer toast to wire rack. Line 9" by 5" metal loaf pan with foil, allowing foil to extend 2 inches above sides.

2. From lemon, grate 1$^1/_2$ teaspoons peel and squeeze 1 tablespoon juice.

3. In 12-inch skillet, melt butter over medium-high heat. Add carrots and onion and cook, stirring occasionally, until onion is tender, 6 to 7 minutes. Add zucchini and cook until vegetables are tender, 4 to 5 minutes. Remove skillet from heat; stir in $^1/_2$ teaspoon salt and $^1/_2$ teaspoon lemon peel. Cool slightly.

4. Meanwhile, into large bowl, tear remaining bread slices into small pieces. Add chicken, eggs, pepper, and $^1/_2$ teaspoon salt; mix just until well combined. Stir in zucchini mixture.

5. Spoon chicken mixture into prepared pan. Cover pan with foil and bake meat loaf 30 minutes.

6. Meanwhile, prepare gremolata crumbs: In food processor with knife blade attached, pulse garlic until finely chopped. Break toast into pieces and add to processor with parsley; pulse until coarsely chopped. Stir in oil, lemon juice, remaining 1 teaspoon lemon peel, and remaining $^1/_4$ teaspoon salt.

7. Remove and discard foil from top of meat loaf. Spoon gremolata crumbs over meat loaf. Bake, uncovered, until meat thermometer inserted in center of meat loaf reaches 165°F and crumbs are browned, about 20 minutes longer. (Internal temperature will rise to 170°F upon standing.) Let stand 5 minutes to set juices for easier slicing. Using edges of foil to lift meat loaf, remove from pan and transfer to warm platter to serve. Discard foil.

EACH SERVING About 240 calories | 13g protein | 11g carbohydrate | 16g total fat (2g saturated) | 61mg cholesterol | 521mg sodium.

Chicken Shepherd's Pie

Shepherd's pie was originally created as a way to utilize Sunday supper leftovers. We've lightened the ingredients and topped it off with a mantle of creamy, smooth, chive-studded potatoes.

PREP 45 minutes **BAKE** 20 minutes **MAKES** 6 main-dish servings.

2 pounds all-purpose potatoes
  (6 medium), peeled and cut into
  1-inch pieces

2 tablespoons vegetable oil

2 carrots, peeled and finely chopped

1 large onion (12 ounces),
  finely chopped

1 large red pepper, finely chopped

2 tablespoons butter or margarine

1 teaspoon salt

3/4 cup milk

2 tablespoons chopped fresh chives
  or green-onion tops

10 ounces mushrooms, trimmed and
  thickly sliced

1 1/4 cups chicken broth

1 tablespoon all-purpose flour

1 1/2 pounds ground chicken meat

1/4 teaspoon coarsely ground
  black pepper

1/4 teaspoon dried thyme

2 tablespoons ketchup

1 tablespoon Worcestershire sauce

1. In 3-quart saucepan, combine potatoes and enough *water* to cover; heat to boiling over high heat. Reduce heat; cover and simmer until potatoes are tender, about 15 minutes.

2. Meanwhile, in 12-inch skillet, heat 1 tablespoon oil over medium-high heat. Add carrots and cook 5 minutes. Add onion and red pepper and cook, stirring occasionally, until vegetables are tender and lightly browned, about 10 minutes longer. With slotted spoon, transfer vegetables to bowl.

3. When potatoes are tender, drain. Mash potatoes in saucepan with butter and 1/2 teaspoon salt. Gradually add milk; mash until mixture is smooth and well blended. Stir in chives; set aside.

4. In same skillet, heat remaining 1 tablespoon oil over medium-high heat. Add mushrooms and cook until well browned, about 10 minutes. Transfer to bowl with vegetables.

5. In small bowl or cup, blend broth and flour until smooth; set aside.

6. Preheat oven to 400°F. In same skillet, cook ground chicken, black pepper, thyme, and remaining ½ teaspoon salt over high heat, stirring occasionally, until chicken is lightly browned and any liquid in skillet has evaporated, 7 to 10 minutes. Stir in ketchup, Worcestershire, cooked vegetables, and broth mixture. Cook, stirring constantly, until liquid has thickened and boils, 3 to 5 minutes.

7. Spoon chicken mixture into shallow 2-quart casserole; top with mashed potatoes. Place casserole on foil-lined cookie sheet to catch any overflow during baking. Bake until potato topping is lightly browned, 20 to 25 minutes.

EACH SERVING About 415 calories | **26g protein** | **33g carbohydrate** | **20g total fat (6g saturated)** | **109mg cholesterol** | **848mg sodium.**

Chicken Mornay over English Muffins

Gruyère is a rich, nutty-tasting cheese originally from Switzerland. If you can't find it in your market, try a combination of Swiss and Parmesan. This will give the sauce the robust flavor that you want.

PREP 10 minutes **COOK** 10 minutes **MAKES** 4 main-dish servings.

1½ cups whole milk

1 tablespoon cornstarch

1 cup cherry tomatoes

3 cups bite-size pieces cooked chicken (12 ounces)

4 ounces Gruyère cheese

1 small bunch fresh chives, cut into 1-inch pieces (¼ cup)

1 teaspoon chopped fresh thyme or ¼ teaspoon dried thyme

¼ teaspoon salt

⅛ teaspoon ground red pepper (cayenne)

4 English muffins, split and toasted

1. In 10-inch skillet or 3-quart saucepan, with wire whisk, mix milk and cornstarch until blended; heat to boiling over high heat, stirring frequently. Reduce heat to medium and cook, stirring constantly, until sauce has thickened slightly, about 1 minute.

2. Meanwhile, slice each cherry tomato in half and coarsely shred Gruyère.

3. When sauce is ready, add tomatoes, chicken, cheese, chives, thyme, salt, and ground red pepper. With heat-safe spatula or wooden spoon, stir mixture over medium-high heat until heated through.

4. To serve, place 2 English muffin halves on each of 4 dinner plates. Spoon chicken mixture on top.

EACH SERVING About 460 calories | **42g protein** | **33g carbohydrate** | **16g total fat (8g saturated)** | **116mg cholesterol** | **605mg sodium.**

Chicken Enchiladas

These enchiladas in green chile sauce are so tempting you may find yourself roasting a big bird just to have enough leftovers to make them or you can pick up a rotisserie chicken at the grocery store.

PREP 15 minutes **BAKE** 20 minutes **MAKES** 4 main-dish servings.

1 can (4 to 4½ ounces) chopped mild green chiles, undrained

¾ cup loosely packed fresh cilantro leaves and stems

3 green onions, trimmed and sliced

2 tablespoons sliced pickled jalapeño chiles

2 tablespoons fresh lime juice

¼ teaspoon salt

⅓ cup water

4 (8-inch) flour tortillas

2 cups shredded, cooked chicken (8 ounces)

¼ cup heavy or whipping cream

3 ounces Monterey Jack cheese, shredded (¾ cup)

1. Preheat oven to 350°F. Grease 11" by 7" baking dish.

2. In blender, combine chiles, cilantro, green onions, jalapeños, lime juice, salt, and water; puree until smooth. Transfer mixture to 8-inch skillet and heat to boiling over medium heat; boil 2 minutes. Dip one side of each tortilla in sauce; spread 1 tablespoon sauce over other (dry) side of tortilla and top with chicken. Roll up tortilla and place, seam side down, in prepared baking dish.

3. Stir cream into remaining sauce in skillet; spoon over filled tortillas. Cover with foil and bake 15 minutes. Remove foil; sprinkle with cheese and bake until cheese has melted, about 5 minutes longer.

EACH SERVING About 402 calories | 30g protein | 23g carbohydrate | 21g total fat (9g saturated) | 106mg cholesterol | 713mg sodium.

Sautés & Stir-Fries

Thai Chicken with Asparagus
recipe on page 92

Chicken Breasts with Tarragon Sauce

Very popular in French cooking, tarragon has a distinctive licoricelike flavor. If you have leftover fresh tarragon, steep it for a week or so in white wine vinegar; strain and return to the bottle. Use for salad dressings or sweeten and toss with berries.

PREP 10 minutes **COOK** 20 minutes **MAKES** 4 main-dish servings.

2 teaspoons plus I tablespoon olive or vegetable oil

2 large shallots, thinly sliced

5 tablespoons all-purpose flour

I tablespoon fresh tarragon leaves, chopped, or ½ teaspoon dried tarragon

I teaspoon salt

4 large bone-in chicken breast halves (2½ pounds), skin removed

1½ cups chicken broth

1. In nonstick 12-inch skillet, heat 2 teaspoons olive oil over medium heat. Add shallots and cook until tender and lightly browned. With slotted spoon, transfer shallots to bowl.

2. On waxed paper, mix 3 tablespoons flour, tarragon, and salt; use to coat chicken breasts.

3. Add remaining 1 tablespoon oil to skillet and heat until very hot. Add chicken breasts and cook until golden brown, turning once. Reduce heat to medium-low; cover and continue cooking until juices run clear when thickest part of chicken is pierced with tip of knife, about 10 minutes. Transfer chicken to 4 dinner plates.

4. In small bowl, with fork, mix remaining 2 tablespoons flour with chicken broth. Add broth mixture and sautéed shallots to skillet; heat to boiling over high heat, stirring to loosen any brown bits from bottom of skillet. Boil 1 minute. Pour sauce over chicken.

EACH SERVING About 305 calories | 44g protein | 9g carbohydrate | 9g total fat (2g saturated) | 107mg cholesterol | 1,100mg sodium.

Skillet Chicken Parmesan

We sautéed thinly sliced chicken breasts in just a teaspoon of olive oil and used part-skim mozzarella to lighten up this family favorite. Ready-made spaghetti sauce makes this a great weeknight recipe.

PREP 10 minutes **COOK** 10 minutes **MAKES** 4 main-dish servings.

1 teaspoon olive oil

1 pound thinly sliced skinless, boneless chicken breasts

1 container (15 ounces) refrigerated marinara sauce

1 cup shredded part-skim mozzarella cheese (4 ounces)

2 plum tomatoes, chopped

2 tablespoons grated Parmesan cheese

1 cup loosely packed fresh basil leaves, sliced

1. In nonstick 12-inch skillet, heat oil over medium-high heat until hot. Add half of chicken to skillet and cook, turning once, until chicken loses its pink color throughout, about 4 minutes. Transfer cooked chicken to plate; repeat with remaining chicken.

2. Reduce heat to medium. Return chicken to skillet; top with marinara sauce and mozzarella. Cover skillet and cook until sauce is heated through and mozzarella has melted, about 2 minutes. Sprinkle with tomatoes, Parmesan, and basil.

EACH SERVING About 295 calories | 36g protein | 10g carbohydrate | 11g total fat (4g saturated) | 84mg cholesterol | 660mg sodium.

Thai Chicken with Asparagus

Ginger, chiles, and Asian fish sauce turn up the heat in this weeknight dish. If you prefer, use fresh green beans instead of asparagus.

PREP 25 minutes **COOK** 30 minutes **MAKES** 4 main-dish servings.

1 teaspoon salt

1 pound thin asparagus, trimmed and cut diagonally into 3-inch pieces

3 tablespoons Asian fish sauce (nuoc nam)

2 tablespoons fresh lime juice

1 tablespoon plus 1 teaspoon soy sauce

1 tablespoon sugar

4 skinless, boneless chicken breast halves (1¼ pounds), thinly sliced

3 teaspoons vegetable oil

1 jumbo onion (1 pound), thinly sliced

1 piece fresh ginger (2" by 1"), peeled and cut into matchstick strips

2 jalapeño chiles, seeded and cut into matchstick strips

2 cups packed fresh basil leaves

1 cup packed fresh cilantro leaves

1. In 10-inch skillet, heat *1 inch water* and salt to boiling over high heat. Add asparagus; heat to boiling. Reduce heat to low; simmer, uncovered, until asparagus is just tender-crisp, 3 to 5 minutes. Drain asparagus; set aside.

2. In medium bowl, mix fish sauce, lime juice, soy sauce, and sugar. Stir in chicken until evenly coated. (Coat chicken just before cooking because the lime juice will change its texture).

3. In nonstick 12-inch skillet, heat 2 teaspoons oil over medium-high heat until hot. Add chicken and cook, stirring occasionally, just until it loses its pink color throughout, about 5 minutes. With tongs or slotted spoon, transfer chicken to bowl, leaving any cooking liquid in skillet.

4. Add onion, ginger, and jalapeños to skillet and cook until onion is tender, about 8 minutes. Transfer onion mixture to bowl with chicken.

5. In same skillet, heat remaining 1 teaspoon oil over medium heat until hot. Add asparagus to skillet and cook, stirring occasionally, until it begins

to brown, about 5 minutes. Return onion mixture and chicken to skillet; heat through.

6. Toss basil and cilantro leaves with chicken mixture just before serving.

EACH SERVING About 290 calories | 38g protein | 21g carbohydrate | 6g total fat (1g saturated) | 82mg cholesterol | 1,555mg sodium.

Asian Fish Sauce

Asian fish sauce is an integral flavoring in Southeast Asian cooking. It is made from fermented fish. Also know as *nam pla* (Thailand) and *nuoc nam* (Vietnam); the Philippine version, pastis, has a much milder flavor. Store at cool room temperature in a dark place; it will keep for about one year. Fish sauce is available in specialty sections of some supermarkets or in Asian groceries.

Cutlets Romano with Arugula Salad

A flavor-packed coating of bread crumbs and grated cheese quickly transforms ordinary chicken breasts.

PREP 25 minutes **COOK** 8 minutes **MAKES** 4 main-dish servings.

ARUGULA SALAD

2 tablespoons fresh lemon juice

I tablespoon olive oil

$1/2$ teaspoon sugar

$1/8$ teaspoon salt

$1/8$ teaspoon coarsely ground black pepper

I jar (7 ounces) roasted red peppers, drained and thinly sliced

2 bags (3 to 4 ounces each) arugula or I bag (about 6 ounces) baby spinach

CHICKEN CUTLETS

$1/2$ cup plain dried bread crumbs

$1/3$ cup grated Romano cheese

$1/4$ teaspoon salt

$1/4$ teaspoon coarsely ground black pepper

I large egg

4 small skinless, boneless chicken breast halves (I pound), pounded to $1/4$-inch thickness

I tablespoon olive oil

lemon wedges

1. Prepare salad: In large bowl, with wire whisk or fork, mix lemon juice, oil, sugar, salt, and pepper. Add red peppers and toss to coat; place arugula on top and set aside.

2. Prepare cutlets: On waxed paper, combine bread crumbs, Romano cheese, salt, and pepper. In pie plate, beat egg with fork. Dip chicken cutlets into egg, then into crumb mixture, coating both sides.

3. In nonstick 12-inch skillet, heat $1^1/2$ teaspoons oil over medium-high heat until hot. Add half of cutlets and cook just until chicken is golden brown and loses its pink color throughout, about 2 minutes per side; repeat with remaining oil and cutlets.

4. To serve, toss salad and spoon onto 4 dinner plates. Arrange cutlets on top of salad. Serve with lemon wedges.

EACH SERVING About 320 calories | 34g protein | 17g carbohydrate | 13g total fat (3g saturated) | 128mg cholesterol | 665mg sodium.

Peachy Chicken with Basil

Combine fragrant basil and juicy fruit slices in a perfect sauce for sautéed chicken breasts. Spoon over noodles or rice, so you get every drop.

PREP 20 minutes **COOK** 15 minutes **MAKES** 4 main-dish servings.

3 tablespoons all-purpose flour	3 medium peaches (1 pound), peeled and sliced
1/2 teaspoon salt	1 small red onion, thinly sliced
1/2 teaspoon coarsely ground black pepper	1/4 teaspoon freshly grated lemon peel
4 medium skinless, boneless chicken breast halves (1 1/4 pounds)	8 large basil leaves, thinly sliced
2 tablespoons butter or margarine	cooked noodles or rice (optional)
3/4 cup chicken broth	

1. On waxed paper, mix flour, salt, and pepper; use flour mixture to coat chicken, shaking off excess.

2. In nonstick 12-inch skillet, melt butter over medium heat. Add chicken and cook, turning once, until chicken loses its pink color throughout, 10 to 12 minutes. Transfer chicken to platter; keep warm.

3. Add broth to skillet; heat to boiling over high heat. Add peaches, red onion, and lemon peel; cook, stirring frequently, until peaches have softened and sauce has slightly thickened, about 3 minutes. Stir in sliced basil.

4. To serve, arrange chicken on plates with cooked noodles or rice, if using. Spoon sauce over chicken.

EACH SERVING (WITHOUT NOODLES OR RICE) About 280 calories | 35g protein | 16g carbohydrate | 8g total fat (5g saturated) | 98mg cholesterol | 562mg sodium.

Chicken Breasts with Cranberry-Balsamic Sauce and Brussels Sprouts

When it's peak season for cranberries, buy extra and freeze in their original bag for use year-round. No need to thaw; just measure and use.

PREP 10 minutes **COOK** 20 minutes **MAKES** 4 main-dish servings.

I container (10 ounces) Brussels sprouts

I tablespoon plus I teaspoon olive oil

I teaspoon salt

¹/₄ teaspoon ground black pepper

2 tablespoons all-purpose flour

4 medium skinless, boneless chicken breast halves (1¹/₄ pounds)

2 cups cranberries

³/₄ cup water

¹/₄ cup sugar

¹/₄ cup balsamic vinegar

1. Preheat oven to 450°F. Trim Brussels sprouts; cut lengthwise into thin slices. In 15¹/₂" by 10¹/₂" jelly-roll pan, toss sprouts with 1 tablespoon oil, ¹/₂ teaspoon salt, and ¹/₈ teaspoon pepper to coat. Spread evenly in pan; roast until tender and browned at edges, 15 to 20 minutes.

2. Meanwhile, in nonstick 12-inch skillet, heat remaining 1 teaspoon oil over medium-high heat until hot. On waxed paper, combine flour and remaining ¹/₂ teaspoon salt and ¹/₈ teaspoon pepper; use to coat chicken.

3. Add chicken to skillet and cook 6 minutes. Reduce heat to medium; turn chicken and cook until chicken loses its pink color throughout, 6 to 8 minutes longer. Transfer chicken to platter; keep warm.

4. To skillet, add cranberries, water, sugar, and vinegar; heat to boiling over medium-high heat. Cook until sauce thickens slightly, about 5 minutes. Serve chicken with sauce and Brussels sprouts.

EACH SERVING About 320 calories | 36g protein | 30g carbohydrate | 7g total fat (1g saturated) | 82mg cholesterol | 690mg sodium.

Chicken with Pears and Marsala

Fresh pears and a wine sauce spiked with sage transform basic chicken breasts into an elegant main course.

PREP 10 minutes **COOK** 15 minutes **MAKES** 4 main-dish servings.

I teaspoon vegetable oil

4 small skinless, boneless chicken breast halves (I pound)

¹/₄ teaspoon salt

¹/₈ teaspoon ground black pepper

2 Bosc or Anjou pears, each peeled, cored, and quartered

³/₄ cup chicken broth

¹/₂ cup dry Marsala wine

I tablespoon cornstarch

2 teaspoons chopped fresh sage leaves

1. In nonstick 10-inch skillet, heat oil over medium-high heat until hot. Add chicken; sprinkle with salt and pepper. Cook, turning once, until chicken loses its pink color throughout, 10 to 12 minutes. Transfer to plate; keep warm.

2. To skillet, add pears and cook until browned on all sides, 3 to 5 minutes. Meanwhile, in cup, whisk broth, wine, cornstarch, and sage until blended.

3. Carefully add broth mixture to skillet; boil 1 minute to thicken slightly. Return chicken with any juices to skillet; heat through.

EACH SERVING About 195 calories | 27g protein | 12g carbohydrate | 3g total fat (1g saturated) | 66mg cholesterol | 410mg sodium.

Chicken Breasts à l'Orange

Using chicken breasts instead of duck makes short work of this French classic without sacrificing flavor.

PREP 5 minutes **COOK** 15 minutes **MAKES** 4 main-dish servings.

- 1 box (6 ounces) quick-cooking long-grain and wild rice mix
- 1 tablespoon butter or margarine
- 4 medium skinless, boneless chicken breast halves (1¼ pounds)
- ½ teaspoon salt
- 2 medium oranges
- ⅓ cup sweet orange marmalade
- 2 tablespoons red wine vinegar
- 1 teaspoon cornstarch
- 1 small garlic clove, thinly sliced

1. Prepare rice mix as label directs.

2. Meanwhile, in nonstick 10-inch skillet, melt butter over medium-high heat. Add chicken breasts; sprinkle with ¼ teaspoon salt and cook 5 minutes. Reduce heat to medium; turn chicken and cook until chicken loses its pink color throughout, 5 to 7 minutes longer. Transfer chicken to plate; keep warm.

3. While chicken is cooking, from 1 orange, grate ¼ teaspoon peel. Squeeze ½ cup juice into medium bowl. Cut peel and white pith from second orange. Holding orange over same bowl to catch juice, cut sections from between membranes and add to bowl. Squeeze membrane to release any excess juice. You should have at least ¾ cup orange juice and sections. Stir in marmalade, vinegar, cornstarch, orange peel, and remaining ¼ teaspoon salt.

4. Add garlic to drippings in skillet; cook, stirring, 15 seconds. Add orange-juice mixture; heat to boiling. Boil until sauce thickens slightly, about 3 minutes. Return chicken with any juices to skillet; heat through, turning to coat with sauce.

EACH SERVING WITHOUT RICE About 280 calories | 34g protein | 26g carbohydrate | 5g total fat (2g saturated) | 90mg cholesterol | 426mg sodium.

Lemon-Rosemary Chicken

Long on flavor and short on prep time, this dish is a great weeknight entree. Serve with creamy polenta or mashed potatoes.

PREP 10 minutes   **COOK** 10 minutes   **MAKES** 4 main-dish servings.

2 medium lemons

1 tablespoon chopped fresh rosemary or 1/2 teaspoon dried rosemary, crushed

2 teaspoons olive oil

1/2 teaspoon salt

1/4 teaspoon coarsely ground black pepper

1 garlic clove, minced

4 small skinless, boneless chicken breast halves (1 pound)

1. From 1 lemon, grate 2 teaspoons peel. Thinly slice half of second lemon; reserve slices for garnish. Squeeze juice from remaining 3 lemon halves into small bowl. Stir in lemon peel, rosemary, olive oil, salt, pepper, and garlic.

2. Spray heavy 12-inch skillet with nonstick cooking spray. Heat skillet over medium-high heat until very hot.

3. Meanwhile, toss chicken breasts with lemon-juice mixture.

4. Place chicken breasts in hot skillet; cook, brushing with remaining lemon-juice mixture, 5 minutes. Turn chicken and cook until chicken loses its pink color throughout, about 5 minutes longer. Garnish with lemon slices.

EACH SERVING About 155 calories | 27g protein | 3g carbohydrate | 4g total fat (1g saturated) | 66mg cholesterol | 365mg sodium.

Chicken Breasts with Mushrooms and Tarragon

Fast and flavorful, this delicious blend of mushrooms and herbs makes chicken breasts festive enough for special dinner guests.

PREP 20 minutes **COOK** 25 minutes **MAKES** 6 main-dish servings.

2 tablespoons olive oil

1 pound assorted mushrooms (white and cremini, trimmed and sliced; shiitake, stems removed and caps sliced)

1 large shallot, finely chopped

3 tablespoons all-purpose flour

2 tablespoons chopped fresh tarragon or 1 teaspoon dried tarragon

1/2 teaspoon salt

1/4 teaspoon ground black pepper

6 small skinless, boneless chicken breast halves (1 1/2 pounds)

1 cup chicken broth

1/4 cup dry white wine

1. In 12-inch skillet, heat 1 tablespoon oil over medium-high heat. Add mushrooms and shallot and cook, stirring occasionally, until mushrooms are golden brown and any liquid has evaporated, 12 to 15 minutes. Transfer mushroom mixture to bowl.

2. On waxed paper, combine flour, 1 tablespoon chopped tarragon, salt, and pepper; use flour mixture to coat chicken, shaking off excess.

3. In same skillet, heat remaining 1 tablespoon oil over medium-high heat until very hot. Add chicken and cook until chicken is golden brown and loses its pink color throughout, about 4 minutes per side. Transfer chicken to warm platter.

4. Add broth, wine, remaining 1 tablespoon chopped tarragon, and mushroom mixture to skillet; cook, stirring until browned bits are loosened from bottom of skillet, 1 minute. Pour sauce over chicken.

EACH SERVING About 212 calories | 29g protein | 7g carbohydrate | 7g total fat (1g saturated) | 66mg cholesterol | 437mg sodium.

Chicken Roulades

Butterflying is a cutting technique in which food is cut horizontally almost in half, then opened flat, resembling a butterfly.

PREP 30 minutes   **COOK** 20 minutes   **MAKES** 4 main-dish servings.

4 medium skinless, boneless chicken
  breast halves (1 1/4 pounds)

1/2 (7-ounce) jar roasted red
  peppers, drained and sliced

2 ounces herb-and-garlic goat cheese

1/2 cup loosely packed basil leaves

1/4 teaspoon salt

1/4 teaspoon coarsely ground
  black pepper

1 tablespoon olive oil

1. Holding knife parallel to cutting surface and against one long side of a chicken breast half, cut chicken almost in half, making sure not to cut all the way through. Open chicken breast half and spread flat like a book. With meat mallet, or between two sheets of plastic wrap or waxed paper with rolling pin, pound chicken breast half to 1/4-inch thickness. Repeat with remaining chicken.

2. Place one-fourth each of red pepper slices, goat cheese, and basil leaves on each breast half. Starting from one long side, roll each breast half jelly-roll fashion; secure with toothpicks. Sprinkle chicken roulades with salt and pepper.

3. Heat oil in nonstick 12-inch skillet over medium-high heat until very hot. Add chicken and cook until golden on all sides. Reduce heat to medium; cover and cook until chicken loses its pink color throughout, 12 to 15 minutes longer.

4. Transfer chicken to cutting board; discard toothpicks. Cut chicken roulades crosswise on diagonal into 1/2-inch-thick slices. Transfer chicken to platter and serve.

EACH SERVING About 203 calories | **29g protein** | **3g carbohydrate** |
8g total fat (3g saturated) | **81mg cholesterol** | **341mg sodium.**

Chicken Breasts with Pecan Crust

These irresistibly crisp chicken breasts deliver plenty of maple flavor and pecan crunch in every bite.

PREP 15 minutes   **COOK** 10 minutes   **MAKES** 4 main-dish servings.

4 medium skinless, boneless chicken breast halves (1¼ pounds)

2 tablespoons maple or maple-flavored syrup

½ cup pecans, finely chopped

½ cup plain dried bread crumbs

¾ teaspoon salt

1 tablespoon butter or margarine

2 tablespoons vegetable oil

1. Brush chicken on both sides with maple syrup. On waxed paper, combine chopped pecans, bread crumbs, and salt; use mixture to coat chicken, firmly pressing so mixture adheres.

2. In nonstick 12-inch skillet, melt butter with oil over medium-high heat. Add chicken and cook until chicken is golden brown and loses its pink color throughout, about 6 minutes per side.

EACH SERVING About 411 calories | 36g protein | 19g carbohydrate | 21g total fat (4g saturated) | 90mg cholesterol | 675mg sodium.

New Chicken Cordon Bleu

A zesty balsamic pan sauce adds a quick flavor boost to this updated classic.

PREP 10 minutes **COOK** 20 minutes **MAKES** 4 main-dish servings.

1 tablespoon butter or margarine	4 thin slices cooked ham (2 ounces)
4 small skinless, boneless chicken breast halves (1 pound)	4 thin slices part-skim mozzarella cheese (2 ounces)
½ cup chicken broth	1 bag (5 to 6 ounces) prewashed baby spinach
2 tablespoons balsamic vinegar	
⅛ teaspoon coarsely ground black pepper	

1. In nonstick 12-inch skillet, melt butter over medium-high heat. Add chicken and cook until golden brown, about 6 minutes. Turn chicken and reduce heat to medium; cover and cook until chicken loses its pink color throughout, about 6 minutes longer.

2. Increase heat to medium-high. Stir in broth, vinegar, and pepper; cook, uncovered, 1 minute. Remove skillet from heat; top each breast half with ham slice, then cheese slice. Cover skillet until cheese melts, about 3 minutes.

3. Arrange spinach on warm platter. With spatula, arrange chicken on top of spinach; drizzle with balsamic mixture.

EACH SERVING About 224 calories | 34g protein | 2g carbohydrate | 8g total fat (4g saturated) | 90mg cholesterol | 535mg sodium.

Chicken Parmigiana

Smothered in marinara sauce and topped with mozzarella cheese, this Italian-restaurant favorite is easy to make at home.

PREP 30 minutes **COOK** 25 minutes **MAKES** 6 main-dish servings.

2 cups Marinara Sauce (page 111) or bottled marinara sauce

1 cup plain dried bread crumbs

1/2 teaspoon salt

1/8 teaspoon ground black pepper

1 large egg

2 tablespoons water

6 small skinless, boneless chicken breast halves (1 1/2 pounds)

3 tablespoons butter or margarine

1/4 cup freshly grated Parmesan cheese

4 ounces part-skim mozzarella cheese, shredded (1 cup)

1. Prepare Marinara Sauce, if using.

2. On waxed paper, combine bread crumbs, salt, and pepper. In pie plate, beat egg and water. Dip cutlets in egg mixture, then in bread crumbs; repeat to coat each cutlet twice.

3. In 12-inch skillet, melt butter over medium heat. Add cutlets, a few at a time, and cook until browned, about 5 minutes per side, using slotted spatula to transfer cutlets to platter as they are browned.

4. Return cutlets to skillet. Spoon sauce evenly over cutlets. Sprinkle with Parmesan and top with mozzarella. Reduce heat to low; cover and cook just until cheese has melted, about 5 minutes.

EACH SERVING About 419 calories | 39g protein | 30g carbohydrate | 16g total fat (8g saturated) | 131mg cholesterol | 1,388mg sodium.

Marinara Sauce

In nonreactive 3-quart saucepan, heat **2 tablespoons olive oil** over medium heat. Add **1 small onion**, chopped, and **1 garlic clove**, finely chopped; cook, stirring, until onion is tender, about 5 minutes. Stir in **1 can (28 ounces) plum tomatoes** with their juice, **2 tablespoons tomato paste**, **2 tablespoons chopped fresh basil or parsley**, if using, and **¹/₂ teaspoon salt**. Heat to boiling, breaking up tomatoes with side of spoon. Reduce heat; partially cover and simmer, stirring occasionally, until sauce has thickened slightly, about 20 minutes. Makes 3¹/₂ cups.

EACH ¹/₂ CUP **About 67 calories** I **1g protein** I **7g carbohydrate** I **4g total fat (1g saturated)** I **0mg cholesterol** I **388mg sodium.**

Peanut Chicken

This exotic dish is based on the cuisine of West Africa. Serve with a crisp cucumber salad and steamed white or brown rice.

PREP 10 minutes **COOK** 10 minutes **MAKES** 4 main-dish servings.

1 can (14½ ounces) diced tomatoes	¼ teaspoon crushed red pepper
¼ cup packed fresh cilantro leaves	1 teaspoon ground cumin
¼ cup creamy peanut butter	¼ teaspoon ground cinnamon
2 garlic cloves, peeled	1 pound chicken breast tenders
½ teaspoon salt	1 tablespoon vegetable oil

1. Drain tomatoes and reserve juice. In blender at high speed or in food processor with knife blade attached, puree tomato juice, cilantro, peanut butter, garlic, salt, and crushed red pepper until smooth.

2. In medium bowl, mix cumin and cinnamon; stir in chicken tenders.

3. In nonstick 12-inch skillet, heat vegetable oil over medium-high heat until hot. Add chicken and cook, turning once, until browned, about 5 minutes.

4. Pour peanut butter mixture and diced tomatoes over chicken; heat to boiling. Reduce heat to low; simmer, uncovered, 5 minutes to blend flavors.

EACH SERVING About 275 calories | 32g protein | 8g carbohydrate | 13g total fat (2g saturated) | 66mg cholesterol | 610mg sodium.

Asian Stir-Fry with Spring Peas

Serve over fluffy white rice for a simple any-day supper.

PREP 20 minutes **COOK** 20 minutes **MAKES** 4 main-dish servings.

- 1 pound chicken breast tenders
- ½ teaspoon Chinese five-spice powder
- ¼ teaspoon salt
- 3 teaspoons vegetable oil
- 8 ounces snow peas and/or sugar snap peas, strings removed
- 1 medium red pepper, thinly sliced
- 2 tablespoons water
- 1 cup chicken broth

- 1 tablespoon dark brown sugar
- 1 tablespoon soy sauce
- 2 teaspoons cornstarch
- 2 green onions, trimmed and cut into ½-inch pieces
- 1 tablespoon grated, peeled fresh ginger
- 2 garlic cloves, crushed with garlic press

1. On waxed paper, sprinkle chicken with Chinese five-spice powder and salt. In nonstick 12-inch skillet, heat 1 teaspoon oil over medium-high heat until hot. Add chicken and cook, turning once, just until it loses its pink color throughout, about 5 minutes. Transfer to plate; set aside.

2. To skillet, add remaining 2 teaspoons oil and cook peas and red pepper, stirring occasionally, about 5 minutes. Add water. Cover and cook, stirring occasionally, until vegetables are tender-crisp, about 3 minutes.

3. Meanwhile, in small bowl, mix broth, brown sugar, soy sauce, and cornstarch.

4. Add green onions, ginger, and garlic to skillet; cook, stirring, 1 minute. Stir broth mixture, then add to skillet. Heat to boiling; boil 30 seconds. Add chicken and heat through.

EACH SERVING About 220 calories | 30g protein | 12g carbohydrate | 5g total fat (1g saturated) | 66mg cholesterol | 665mg sodium.

Peanut-Chicken Stir-Fry

Delight your family by preparing this popular Chinese dish. Using instant rice, chicken tenders, and prepackaged broccoli flowerets, you'll have it on the table in a flash.

PREP 10 minutes   **COOK** 10 minutes   **MAKES** 4 main-dish servings.

I cup instant brown rice

I cup chicken broth

2 tablespoons soy sauce

I tablespoon brown sugar

I tablespoon cornstarch

2 teaspoons vegetable oil

I pound chicken breast tenders, each cut lengthwise in half if large

I package (12 ounces) broccoli flowerets

I small red pepper, cut into 1-inch pieces

I small onion, cut in half and sliced

I teaspoon grated, peeled fresh ginger

½ cup unsalted roasted peanuts

I teaspoon Asian sesame oil

1. Prepare rice as label directs.

2. Meanwhile, in cup, stir broth, soy sauce, sugar, and cornstarch until smooth.

3. In nonstick 12-inch skillet, heat oil over medium-high heat until very hot. Add chicken and cook, stirring frequently (stir-frying), until it just loses its pink color throughout, 4 to 5 minutes. Transfer chicken to bowl.

4. To same skillet, add broccoli, red pepper, onion, ginger, and ¼ cup broth mixture. Cover skillet and cook, stirring occasionally, until vegetables are tender-crisp, about 3 minutes. Stir remaining broth mixture and add to skillet with chicken and any juices; heat to boiling. Boil until mixture has thickened slightly, about 1 minute. Remove skillet from heat; stir in peanuts and sesame oil.

5. To serve, spoon rice onto 4 dinner plates; top with chicken mixture.

EACH SERVING About 275 calories | 25g protein | 23g carbohydrate | 10g total fat (1g saturated) | 44mg cholesterol | 560mg sodium.

Chicken with Buttermilk Gravy

Tangy buttermilk makes a flavorful addition to this simple pan gravy.

PREP 10 minutes   **COOK** 25 minutes   **MAKES** 4 main-dish servings.

8 large bone-in chicken thighs ($2^{1}/_{2}$ pounds), skin and fat removed

1 cup buttermilk

$^{1}/_{2}$ cup plus 1 tablespoon all-purpose flour

1 teaspoon chopped fresh thyme or $^{1}/_{2}$ teaspoon dried thyme

$^{1}/_{2}$ teaspoon salt

1 tablespoon vegetable oil

1 cup chicken broth

1. In bowl, mix chicken thighs with $^{1}/_{2}$ cup buttermilk. On waxed paper, mix $^{1}/_{2}$ cup flour, thyme, and salt. Use flour mixture to coat thighs.

2. In nonstick 12-inch skillet, heat oil over medium-high heat until very hot. Add chicken thighs and cook until golden. Reduce heat to medium-low; cook, turning chicken occasionally, until juices run clear when thickest part of chicken is pierced with tip of knife, about 15 minutes longer. Transfer chicken to platter.

3. In small bowl, with fork, mix remaining 1 tablespoon flour and broth. Add mixture to skillet, stirring until browned bits are loosened from bottom of pan. Heat over medium-high heat until mixture boils and thickens; boil 1 minute. Remove from heat; stir in remaining $^{1}/_{2}$ cup buttermilk. Serve gravy with chicken.

EACH SERVING About 320 calories | 36g protein | 17g carbohydrate | 11g total fat (3g saturated) | 137mg cholesterol | 755mg sodium.

Chicken Amalfi

Named after a picture-postcard section of Italy's spectacular coastline, this dish is chockful of bold Mediterranean flavor.

PREP 10 minutes **COOK** 40 minutes **MAKES** 4 main-dish servings.

2 tablespoons olive or vegetable oil

4 medium chicken leg quarters (2¹/₄ pounds), separated into drumsticks and thighs, skin removed

¹/₂ teaspoon salt

1 medium onion, thinly sliced

3 medium plum tomatoes, seeded and diced

¹/₄ cup **Kalamata** or **Niçoise** olives, pitted and coarsely chopped

3 tablespoons capers, drained and chopped

¹/₂ cup chicken broth

¹/₂ teaspoon dried rosemary, crushed

2 tablespoons fresh lemon juice

¹/₃ cup water

1 tablespoon chopped fresh parsley leaves

1. In 12-inch skillet, heat oil over medium-high heat until very hot. Add chicken pieces and salt and cook until chicken is golden brown on all sides, transferring chicken pieces to plate as they brown.

2. Add onion to skillet and cook, stirring frequently, until golden. Stir in tomatoes, olives, capers, broth, rosemary, lemon juice, and water.

3. Return chicken to skillet; heat to boiling over high heat. Reduce heat to low; cover and simmer, occasionally spooning olive mixture over chicken, until chicken loses its pink color throughout, 25 to 30 minutes.

4. To serve, arrange chicken pieces on platter and top with olive mixture. Sprinkle with chopped parsley.

EACH SERVING About 290 calories | 30g protein | 8g carbohydrate | 15g total fat (3g saturated) | 116mg cholesterol | 985mg sodium.

Texas Chicken Burgers

The addition of grated zucchini and carrots makes these lowfat chicken burgers light and moist.

PREP 15 minutes **COOK** 12 minutes **MAKES** 4 main-dish servings.

1 pound ground chicken meat

2 green onions, trimmed and chopped

1 small zucchini, grated

1 carrot, peeled and grated

1 tablespoon chili powder

¾ teaspoon salt

¼ teaspoon ground cumin

⅛ teaspoon ground red pepper (cayenne)

1. In medium bowl, with hands, combine ground chicken, green onions, zucchini, carrot, chili powder, salt, cumin, and ground red pepper just until well blended but not overmixed.

2. On waxed paper, shape ground chicken mixture into four 3½-inch patties, handling meat as little as possible.

3. Grease 12-inch skillet with cooking spray. Heat over medium-high heat until very hot. With spatula, transfer patties to skillet. Cook 6 minutes; turn patties and cook until they have lost their pink color throughout, about 6 minutes longer.

EACH SERVING About 198 calories | 21g protein | 4g carbohydrate | 11g total fat (3g saturated) | 94mg cholesterol | 556mg sodium.

Grills & Broils

Chinese Five-Spice Grilled Chicken
recipe on page 122

Grilled Whole Chicken with Lemon and Garlic

Use a covered grill to cook this deliciously seasoned chicken.

PREP 15 minutes **GRILL** 1 hour 15 minutes **MAKES** 4 main-dish servings.

1 chicken (3¹/₂ pounds)	6 garlic cloves, peeled
1 lemon	¹/₂ teaspoon salt
1 small bunch thyme	¹/₄ teaspoon coarsely ground black pepper

1. Prepare grill. Remove giblets and neck from chicken; reserve for another use. Rinse chicken inside and out with cold running water; drain well. Pat dry with paper towels.

2. From lemon, grate 2 teaspoons peel. Cut lemon into quarters and reserve. Chop enough thyme leaves to equal 1 teaspoon; reserve remaining sprigs. Into cup, crush 2 garlic cloves with garlic press; reserve remaining 4 cloves. To garlic in cup, add lemon peel, chopped thyme, salt, and pepper; set aside. Place lemon quarters, whole garlic cloves, and 3 thyme sprigs inside cavity of chicken.

3. With chicken breast side up, lift wings up toward neck, then fold wing tips under back of chicken so wings stay in place. Tie legs together with string. Rub lemon mixture on outside of chicken.

4. Place chicken on hot grill rack over indirect medium heat; cover and grill chicken 1 hour 15 minutes. Chicken is done when temperature on meat thermometer inserted into thickest part of thigh, next to body, reaches 175° to 180°F and juices run clear when thickest part of thigh is pierced with tip of knife.

5. Place chicken on platter; let stand 10 minutes to set juices for easier carving. Remove skin from chicken before eating if you like.

EACH SERVING WITHOUT SKIN About 235 calories | 36g protein | 1g carbohydrate | 9g total fat (3g saturated) | 109mg cholesterol | 395mg sodium.

All-American Barbecued Chicken

We like to remove the skin from the chicken before grilling: It reduces the chance of flare-ups.

PREP 1 hour **GRILL** 40 minutes **MAKES** 8 main-dish servings.

2 tablespoons olive oil

1 large onion (12 ounces), chopped

2 cans (15 ounces each) tomato sauce

1 cup red wine vinegar

$^1/_2$ cup light (mild) molasses

$^1/_4$ cup Worcestershire sauce

$^1/_3$ cup packed brown sugar

$^3/_4$ teaspoon ground red pepper (cayenne)

2 chickens (3$^1/_2$ pounds each), each cut into quarters and skin removed from all but wings, if desired

1. In nonstick 10-inch skillet, heat oil over medium heat. Add onion and cook until tender, about 5 minutes. Stir in tomato sauce, vinegar, molasses, Worcestershire, brown sugar, and ground red pepper; heat to boiling over high heat. Reduce heat to medium-low and cook, stirring occasionally, until sauce has thickened slightly, about 45 minutes. If not using sauce right away, cover and refrigerate to use within 2 weeks.

2. Prepare grill. Reserve 1½ cups of sauce to serve with chicken. Arrange chicken on hot grill rack over medium heat and grill, turning once, 20 to 25 minutes. Generously brush chicken with some of remaining barbecue sauce and grill, brushing frequently with sauce and turning chicken often, until juices run clear when thickest part of chicken is pierced with tip of knife, about 20 minutes longer. Serve with reserved sauce.

EACH SERVING WITHOUT ADDITIONAL SAUCE, WITH SKIN
About 518 calories | 49g protein | 21g carbohydrate | 26g total fat
(7g saturated) | 154mg cholesterol | 564mg sodium.

EACH SERVING WITHOUT ADDITIONAL SAUCE, WITHOUT SKIN About
370 calories | 42g protein | 21g carbohydrate | 13g total fat (3g saturated) |
127mg cholesterol | 543mg sodium.

EACH $^1/_4$ CUP SAUCE About 99 calories | 1g protein | 20g carbohydrate |
2g total fat (0g saturated) | 0mg cholesterol | 422mg sodium.

Chinese Five-Spice Grilled Chicken

Lots of flavor from just a few ingredients makes this a cinch for outdoor or indoor grilling.

PREP 10 minutes plus marinating **GRILL** 25 minutes **MAKES** 4 main-dish servings.

$^{1}/_{4}$ cup dry sherry

1 tablespoon Asian sesame oil

1 teaspoon Chinese five-spice powder

$^{1}/_{4}$ teaspoon ground red pepper (cayenne)

1 chicken (3$^{1}/_{2}$ pounds), cut into 8 pieces and skin removed from all but wings

$^{1}/_{3}$ cup hoisin sauce

1 tablespoon soy sauce

1 teaspoon sesame seeds

1. In large bowl, stir sherry, sesame oil, five-spice powder, and ground red pepper until blended.

2. Add chicken to spice mixture; toss until evenly coated. Cover bowl and let stand 15 minutes at room temperature, turning chicken occasionally.

3. Prepare grill.

4. Place chicken on hot grill rack over medium heat. Cover and grill, turning pieces once and transferring to platter as they are done, until juices run clear when thickest part of chicken is pierced with tip of knife, 20 to 25 minutes.

5. In small bowl, mix hoisin sauce and soy sauce. Brush hoisin-sauce mixture all over chicken and return to grill. Grill, turning once, until glazed, 4 to 5 minutes longer. Transfer chicken to same platter; sprinkle with sesame seeds.

EACH SERVING About 350 calories | 41g protein | 10g carbohydrate | 15g total fat (4g saturated) | 121mg cholesterol | 595mg sodium.

Citrus-Sage Chicken

Sage makes an excellent addition to a garden or window box. It doesn't require much attention and grows more lush and beautiful each year. At summer's end, tie sprigs in bunches and hang upside down in a cool, dark place to dry.

PREP 25 minutes plus marinating   **GRILL** 30 minutes   **MAKES** 8 main-dish servings.

2 large oranges

2 large lemons

1/4 cup chopped fresh sage

2 tablespoons olive oil

2 teaspoons salt

3/4 teaspoon coarsely ground black pepper

2 chickens (3 1/2 pounds each), each cut into 8 pieces and skin removed from all but wings

1. From oranges, grate 1 tablespoon peel and squeeze 3 tablespoons juice. From lemons, grate 1 tablespoon peel and squeeze 3 tablespoons juice.

2. In large bowl, with wire whisk, combine orange and lemon peels and juices, sage, oil, salt, and pepper. Add chicken, turning to coat. Cover and refrigerate chicken 2 hours, turning three or four times.

3. Prepare grill. Arrange chicken, meat side down, on hot grill rack over medium heat and grill 20 minutes. Turn chicken and grill until juices run clear when thickest part of chicken is pierced with tip of knife, 10 to 15 minutes longer.

EACH SERVING About 307 calories | 41g protein | 2g carbohydrate | 14g total fat (3g saturated) | 127mg cholesterol | 705mg sodium.

Grilled Chicken Breasts, Three Ways

This simple recipe for grilled chicken breasts on the bone with crispy skin and juicy meat takes on a new dimension when one of our flavorful mixtures is rubbed under the skin: Sun-Dried Tomato and Basil, Garlic-Herb, or Sage-Butter.

PREP 15 minutes **GRILL** 25 minutes **MAKES** 4 main-dish servings.

choice of Seasoning Mixture (below)	1/2 teaspoon salt
2 large whole bone-in chicken breasts, split (2 1/2 pounds)	1/4 teaspoon coarsely ground black pepper

1. Prepare grill.

2. Prepare one of the seasoning mixtures (below).

3. With fingertips, separate skin from meat on each breast half. Rub equal amounts of Seasoning Mixture under skin of each breast. Sprinkle chicken with salt and pepper.

4. Place chicken on hot grill rack over medium heat and grill, turning once, until juices run clear when thickest part of breast is pierced with tip of knife, about 25 minutes.

Sun-Dried Tomato and Basil Seasoning

In small bowl, mix *2 sun-dried tomatoes packed in seasoned olive oil*, minced, and *1/4 cup loosely packed fresh basil leaves*, finely chopped.

EACH SERVING WITH CHICKEN About 305 calories | 46g protein | 0g carbohydrate | 12g total fat (3g saturated) | 129mg cholesterol | 405mg sodium.

Garlic-Herb Seasoning

In small bowl, mix *2 garlic cloves*, crushed with garlic press, *1 tablespoon chopped fresh rosemary*, *1 tablespoon olive oil*, and 1 *teaspoon freshly grated lemon peel*.

EACH SERVING WITH CHICKEN About 335 calories | 46g protein | 1g carbohydrate | 15g total fat (4g saturated) | 129mg cholesterol | 400mg sodium.

Sage-Butter Seasoning

In small bowl, mix *1 tablespoon butter or margarine*, softened, and *1 tablespoon chopped fresh sage leaves*.

EACH SERVING WITH CHICKEN About 330 calories | 46g protein | 0g carbohydrate | 15g total fat (5g saturated) | 137mg cholesterol | 426mg sodium.

Grilled Basil Chicken with Baby Greens

Fragrant basil leaves turn everyday chicken breasts into something special. If you don't have a grill, roast chicken in the oven at 450°F for about 25 minutes.

PREP 20 minutes **GRILL** 25 minutes **MAKES** 4 main-dish servings.

1 large bunch basil

4 medium bone-in chicken breast halves (2 pounds)

$^3/_4$ teaspoon salt

$^1/_4$ teaspoon coarsely ground black pepper

3 ripe medium tomatoes, chopped

$^1/_4$ cup olive oil

2 tablespoons white wine vinegar

2 teaspoons freshly grated lemon peel

$^1/_2$ teaspoon Dijon mustard

4 ounces mixed baby greens (8 cups) or sliced romaine lettuce leaves

1. Prepare grill.

2. Meanwhile, from bunch of basil, reserve 8 large leaves and measure 1 cup loosely packed small leaves. Finely slice enough remaining leaves to equal $^1/_2$ cup loosely packed. Cover and refrigerate small and sliced leaves.

3. Place 2 reserved large basil leaves under skin of each chicken breast half. Sprinkle chicken with $^1/_4$ teaspoon salt and $^1/_8$ teaspoon pepper. Place breasts, skin side up, on grill over medium heat. Grill chicken, turning once, until juices run clear when thickest part of breast is pierced with tip of knife and skin is brown and crisp, about 25 minutes.

4. Meanwhile, in small bowl, stir tomatoes, oil, vinegar, lemon peel, mustard, remaining $^1/_2$ teaspoon salt, and remaining $^1/_8$ teaspoon pepper.

5. To serve, in large bowl, toss baby greens with small basil leaves. Stir sliced basil leaves into tomato mixture. Toss greens with $^1/_2$ cup tomato mixture. Arrange greens on 4 dinner plates; top with chicken breasts. Spoon remaining tomato mixture over breasts.

EACH SERVING About 340 calories | 31g protein | 6g carbohydrate | 22g total fat (5g saturated) | 83mg cholesterol | 490mg sodium.

Jamaican Jerk Chicken Kabobs

Originally, jerk seasoning was used to season pork shoulder, which was "jerked" apart into shreds before serving. Nowadays, this very popular, power-packed seasoning rub is enjoyed on fish and chicken as well.

PREP 15 minutes plus marinating   BROIL 10 minutes   MAKES 4 main-dish servings.

2 green onions, trimmed
  and chopped

1 jalapeño chile, seeded and minced

1 tablespoon minced, peeled
  fresh ginger

2 tablespoons white wine vinegar

2 tablespoons Worcestershire sauce

3 teaspoons vegetable oil

1 teaspoon ground allspice

1 teaspoon dried thyme

$1/2$ teaspoon plus $1/8$ teaspoon salt

1 pound skinless, boneless chicken
  breast halves, cut into 12 pieces

1 red pepper, cut into 1-inch pieces

1 green pepper, cut into
  1-inch pieces

4 metal skewers

1. In blender or in food processor with knife blade attached, process green onions, jalapeño, ginger, vinegar, Worcestershire, 2 teaspoons oil, allspice, thyme, and ½ teaspoon salt until paste forms.

2. Place chicken in small bowl or in ziptight plastic bag and add green-onion mixture, turning to coat chicken. Cover bowl or seal bag and refrigerate chicken 1 hour.

3. Meanwhile, in small bowl, toss red and green peppers with remaining 1 teaspoon oil and remaining ⅛ teaspoon salt.

4. Preheat broiler. On skewers, alternately thread chicken and pepper pieces.

5. Place kabobs on rack in broiling pan. Brush kabobs with any remaining marinade. Place pan in broiler at closest position to heat source. Broil kabobs 5 minutes; turn and broil until chicken loses its pink color throughout, about 5 minutes longer.

EACH SERVING About 181 calories | 27g protein | 6g carbohydrate | 5g total fat (1g saturated) | 66mg cholesterol | 525mg sodium.

Thai Chicken Saté

Tender slices of skewered chicken are marinated in a curried coconut milk blend. Pickled cucumber makes a perfect partner.

PREP 45 minutes **GRILL** 5 minutes **MAKES** 4 main-dish servings.

12 (12-inch) bamboo skewers

1 English (seedless) cucumber, thinly sliced crosswise

1 1/2 teaspoons salt

1 tablespoon Thai green curry paste

1/4 cup plus 1/3 cup well-stirred unsweetened coconut milk (not cream of coconut)

4 medium skinless, boneless chicken breast halves (1 1/4 pounds), each cut diagonally into 6 strips

1/4 cup creamy peanut butter

1 tablespoon hot water

2 teaspoons soy sauce

1 teaspoon packed dark brown sugar

1/8 teaspoon ground red pepper (cayenne)

1/4 cup rice vinegar

3 tablespoons granulated sugar

2 medium shallots, thinly sliced

1 jalapeño chile, seeds and membrane discarded, minced

1. Place skewers in *water* to cover; let soak at least 30 minutes.

2. While skewers are soaking, in medium bowl, toss cucumber with salt; let stand 30 minutes at room temperature. In another medium bowl, stir curry paste and 1/4 cup coconut milk until blended. Add chicken and turn to coat. Let stand 15 minutes at room temperature, stirring occasionally.

3. Prepare grill.

4. Meanwhile, prepare peanut sauce: In small bowl, with wire whisk, mix peanut butter, hot water, soy sauce, brown sugar, ground red pepper, and remaining 1/3 cup coconut milk until blended and smooth. Transfer sauce to serving bowl. Makes about 2/3 cup.

5. Drain cucumber, discarding liquid in bowl. Pat cucumber dry with paper towels. Return cucumber to bowl; stir in vinegar, granulated sugar, shallots, and jalapeño; refrigerate until ready to serve.

6. Thread 2 chicken strips on each skewer, accordion-style; discard marinade. Place skewers on hot grill rack over medium-high heat. Cover

and grill, turning skewers once, just until chicken loses its pink color throughout, 5 to 8 minutes.

7. Arrange skewers on platter. Serve with peanut sauce and pickled cucumber.

EACH SERVING WITHOUT PEANUT SAUCE About 260 calories ⏐ 34g protein ⏐ 15g carbohydrate ⏐ 6g total fat (3g saturated) ⏐ 90mg cholesterol ⏐ 525mg sodium.

EACH TABLESPOON PEANUT SAUCE About 50 calories ⏐ 2g protein ⏐ 2g carbohydrate ⏐ 5g total fat (2g saturated) ⏐ 0mg cholesterol ⏐ 90mg sodium.

Grilled Chicken Breasts with a Trio of Sauces

It's easy to grill chicken breasts a day or two ahead. Serve cold or at room temperature with one or all of our three complementary sauces: Peach Salsa, Walnut, and Parsley-Caper. If you prefer not to grill, we've included easy oven-poaching directions as well.

PREP 10 minutes **GRILL** 10 minutes **MAKES** 16 main-dish servings.

16 medium skinless, boneless chicken breast halves (5 pounds)

2 tablespoons olive oil

2 teaspoons freshly grated lemon peel

1 teaspoon salt

$^1/_2$ teaspoon coarsely ground black pepper

sauces (below)

1. In large bowl, toss chicken breasts with oil, lemon peel, salt, and pepper until evenly coated.

2. Place chicken on grill over medium heat (in batches if necessary), and grill, turning once, until chicken loses its pink color throughout, 10 to 12 minutes. Transfer chicken to platter; cover and refrigerate up to 2 days if not serving right away.

3. To serve, arrange chicken on platter. Serve with sauces.

EACH SERVING GRILLED CHICKEN ONLY About 190 calories | 33g protein | 0g carbohydrate | 6g total fat (1g saturated) | 90mg cholesterol | 225mg sodium.

Poached Chicken Breasts

Preheat oven to 400°F. In 3-quart saucepan, heat *1 can (14½ ounces) chicken broth (1¾ cups)* and *5½ cups water* to boiling over high heat. Place *16 medium skinless, boneless chicken breast halves (5 pounds)* in single layer in large roasting pan (17" by 11½"); add *2 bay leaves, 2 teaspoons whole black peppercorns,* and *1 lemon*, thinly sliced. Pour boiling broth mixture over chicken; cover pan tightly with foil. Place pan in oven and poach chicken until chicken loses its pink color throughout, about 35 minutes. With tongs, transfer chicken to platter; cover and refrigerate up to 2 days if not serving right away. Reserve broth for another use. Serve with *sauces*. Makes 16 main-dish servings.

EACH SERVING POACHED CHICKEN ONLY About 160 calories | 31g protein | 0g carbohydrate | 3g total fat (1g saturated) | 82mg cholesterol | 90mg sodium.

Peach Salsa

PREP 20 minutes **MAKES** about 6 cups.

8 ripe peaches (3 pounds), peeled, pitted, and coarsely chopped

1 small red pepper, cut into ¼-inch pieces

2 green onions, trimmed and chopped

¼ cup peach or apricot jam

2 tablespoons balsamic vinegar

2 tablespoons olive oil

In large bowl, toss peaches, red pepper, green onions, jam, vinegar, and oil until combined. Cover and refrigerate until ready to serve or up to 2 days.

EACH ¼ CUP About 40 calories | 0g protein | 8g carbohydrate | 1g total fat (0g saturated) | 0mg cholesterol | 2mg sodium.

Walnut Sauce

PREP 15 minutes   **MAKES** about 2½ cups.

2 cups walnuts, toasted

1 small garlic clove

3 slices firm white bread, torn into large pieces

1 cup reduced-sodium chicken broth or broth from Poached Chicken Breasts

⅓ cup reduced-fat sour cream

¾ teaspoon salt

½ teaspoon sweet paprika

⅛ teaspoon ground red pepper (cayenne)

In food processor, with knife blade attached, process toasted walnuts, garlic, and bread until finely ground. Add broth, sour cream, salt, paprika, and ground red pepper and blend until combined. Cover and refrigerate until ready to serve or up to 3 days.

EACH TABLESPOON About 45 calories | 1g protein | 2g carbohydrate | 4g total fat (1g saturated) | 1mg cholesterol | 70mg sodium.

Parsley-Caper Sauce

PREP 15 minutes   **MAKES** about 1 cup.

3 cups packed fresh parsley leaves

⅓ cup olive oil

¼ cup capers, drained

4 teaspoons water

⅛ teaspoon ground red pepper (cayenne)

1 garlic clove

In food processor, with knife blade attached, process parsley, oil, capers, water, ground red pepper, and garlic until very finely chopped. Cover and refrigerate until ready to serve or up to 2 days.

EACH TABLESPOON About 45 calories | 0g protein | 1g carbohydrate | 5g total fat (1g saturated) | 0mg cholesterol | 70mg sodium.

Grilled Chicken Breasts Saltimbocca

In Italian, *saltimbocca* means "jump in your mouth," and these irresistible prosciutto and sage–topped chicken breasts will do just that.

PREP 5 minutes   **GRILL** 10 minutes   **MAKES** 4 main-dish servings.

4 medium skinless, boneless chicken breast halves (1¼ pounds)

⅛ teaspoon salt

⅛ teaspoon ground black pepper

12 fresh sage leaves

4 large slices prosciutto (4 ounces)

1. Prepare grill. Sprinkle chicken with salt and pepper. Place 3 sage leaves on each breast half. Place 1 prosciutto slice on top of each breast half, tucking in edges if necessary; secure with toothpicks.

2. Arrange chicken, prosciutto side down, on hot grill rack over medium heat and grill 5 to 6 minutes. Turn and grill until chicken loses its pink color throughout, 5 to 6 minutes longer.

EACH SERVING About 223 calories | 41g protein | 0g carbohydrate | 6g total fat (1g saturated) | 105mg cholesterol | 690mg sodium.

Chicken with Tomato-Olive Relish

Puttanesca, a piquant Italian pasta sauce, is the inspiration behind grilled chicken breasts topped with a no-cook tomato relish.

PREP 15 minutes   **GRILL** 10 minutes   **MAKES** 4 main-dish servings.

2 medium tomatoes, chopped

¼ cup Kalamata olives, pitted and coarsely chopped, plus additional whole olives

2 tablespoons finely chopped red onion

2 tablespoons capers, drained

3 teaspoons olive oil

1 teaspoon red wine vinegar

4 small skinless, boneless chicken breast halves (1 pound)

¼ teaspoon salt

¼ teaspoon coarsely ground black pepper

1. Prepare grill. In small bowl, combine tomatoes, chopped olives, red onion, capers, 1 teaspoon oil, and vinegar.

2. In medium bowl, sprinkle chicken with salt and pepper and drizzle with remaining 2 teaspoons oil.

3. Arrange chicken on hot grill rack over medium heat and grill until chicken loses its pink color throughout, 5 to 6 minutes per side. Serve chicken topped with tomato-olive relish and garnished with whole olives.

EACH SERVING About 198 calories | 27g protein | 5g carbohydrate | 7g total fat (1g saturated) | 66mg cholesterol | 565mg sodium.

Port and Black Currant–Glazed Chicken Thighs

A robust combination of Port, Dijon mustard, and fresh tarragon makes a delectable quick marinade for these chicken thighs. A last-minute brush with a black currant–jelly glaze adds a glisten.

PREP 15 minutes plus marinating **GRILL** 25 minutes **MAKES** 4 main-dish servings.

1/3 cup ruby **Port**

1/4 cup **Dijon mustard**

1/2 teaspoon **salt**

1/4 teaspoon **coarsely ground black pepper**

2 tablespoons **chopped fresh tarragon leaves**

8 large **chicken thighs (2 1/2 pounds), skin and fat removed**

1/4 cup **black currant jelly**

1. Prepare grill.

2. In large bowl, with wire whisk, mix Port, mustard, salt, pepper, and 1 tablespoon tarragon until blended. Transfer 3 tablespoons marinade to small bowl.

3. Add chicken to marinade remaining in large bowl; toss until evenly coated. Cover bowl and let stand 15 minutes at room temperature or 30 minutes in the refrigerator.

4. Meanwhile, whisk black currant jelly into marinade in small bowl until blended; set aside.

5. Place chicken on hot grill rack over medium heat and grill, turning once, until juices run clear when thickest part of thigh is pierced with tip of knife, about 25 minutes. Brush jelly mixture all over chicken; grill, turning once, until glazed, 1 to 2 minutes longer. Transfer chicken to platter; sprinkle with remaining 1 tablespoon tarragon.

EACH SERVING About 280 calories | 28g protein | 15g carbohydrate | 12g total fat (3g saturated) | 99mg cholesterol | 290mg sodium.

Portuguese Mixed Grill

Here's a colorful and tasty summertime grill. In Portuguese cooking, a vinegar marinade is used to tenderize tough cuts of meat and poultry. We like it for its zesty flavor, since our chicken rarely needs tenderizing.

PREP 30 minutes plus marinating   **GRILL** 25 minutes   **MAKES** 6 main-dish servings.

¼ cup red wine vinegar

2 tablespoons olive oil

2 tablespoons chopped fresh oregano or 1 teaspoon dried oregano

1 teaspoon salt

½ teaspoon coarsely ground black pepper

8 small chicken thighs (1¾ pounds), skin and fat removed

3 medium red onions, each cut into 6 wedges

3 (10-inch) metal skewers

12 ounces fully cooked chorizo sausage links, each cut crosswise in half

⅔ cup assorted olives such as Kalamata, cracked green, and picholine

1. In bowl, combine vinegar, 1 tablespoon oil, 1 tablespoon fresh oregano, salt, and pepper. Add chicken, turning to coat. Cover and refrigerate 30 minutes, no longer.

2. Meanwhile, thread onion wedges onto skewers.

3. Prepare grill. Place onion skewers on hot grill rack over medium heat; brush with remaining 1 tablespoon oil and grill 5 minutes. Arrange chicken on grill rack and grill, turning onions and chicken once, until onions are tender and juices run clear when thickest part of chicken is pierced with tip of knife, about 20 minutes longer.

4. About 10 minutes before onions and chicken are done, place chorizo pieces on grill and cook, turning chorizo occasionally, until lightly browned and heated through.

5. To serve, remove onion wedges from skewers and arrange on warm platter with chicken and chorizo. Scatter olives on top and sprinkle with remaining 1 tablespoon oregano.

EACH SERVING About 482 calories | 34g protein | 11g carbohydrate | 33g total fat (10g saturated) | 130mg cholesterol | 1,495mg sodium.

Five-Spice Chicken Thighs with Plum Chutney

Orange marmalade–basted chicken thighs are complemented by a tangy fresh plum chutney.

PREP 20 minutes plus marinating   **GRILL** 18 minutes   **MAKES** 4 main-dish servings.

PLUM CHUTNEY

1 pound ripe plums
(4 medium), pitted and
cut into $1/4$ -inch pieces

$1/4$ cup lightly packed fresh basil
leaves, chopped

2 tablespoons balsamic vinegar

1 tablespoon minced red onion

2 teaspoons sugar

1 teaspoon grated, peeled
fresh ginger

$1/8$ teaspoon salt

FIVE-SPICE CHICKEN THIGHS

8 small bone-in chicken thighs
(2 pounds), skin and fat removed

1 teaspoon salt

1 garlic clove, crushed with
garlic press

$2^1/2$ teaspoons Chinese five-spice
powder

3 tablespoons orange marmalade

1 tablespoon water

nonstick cooking spray

1. Prepare chutney: In medium bowl, combine plums, basil, vinegar, onion, sugar, ginger, and salt. Cover and refrigerate at least 1 hour or up to 1 day. Makes about $2^1/2$ cups.

2. Meanwhile, prepare grill.

3. Prepare chicken thighs: In medium bowl, toss chicken with salt, garlic, and 2 teaspoons five-spice powder. In cup, mix marmalade with remaining $1/2$ teaspoon five-spice powder and water.

4. Spray chicken with nonstick cooking spray. Place chicken on hot grill rack over medium heat. Cover and grill chicken, turning once, 16 minutes. Brush chicken with half of marmalade mixture; turn chicken and grill, uncovered, 1 minute. Brush chicken with remaining marmalade mixture; turn and grill until juices run clear when thickest part of thigh is pierced with tip of knife, about 1 minute longer. Serve with Plum Chutney.

EACH SERVING CHICKEN ONLY About 290 calories | 27g protein | 11g carbohydrate | 11g total fat (4g saturated) | 99mg cholesterol | 685mg sodium.

EACH ¹/₄ CUP CHUTNEY About 30 calories | 0g protein | 7g carbohydrate | 0g protein | 7g carbohydrate | 0g total fat | 0mg cholesterol | 30mg sodium.

Plums

A luscious, juicy plum is a delectable fruit for eating out of hand, but plums are versatile enough to be used in baked goods, chutneys, relishes, sauces, jams, and jellies. Domestic plums are available from June through September. Buy only ripe fruit—a plum's sweetness does not increase as the fruit softens. Color is determined by variety. Plums should be plump and evenly colored and yield to gentle pressure. If the powdery bloom is still on the skin, it's a sign they haven't been overhandled. Avoid hard, shriveled, or cracked plums.

Greengage plums are a round, very sweet, perfumed fruit with greenish yellow skin. *Damson* and *Mirabelle* plums are members of the same family. *Italian prune* plums are purplish black, oval, freestone plums. Because the flesh is somewhat dry, this plum is best cooked or dried. One of the most popular plum varieties is the *Santa Rosa*. Grown primarily in California, this excellent all-purpose plum has juicy, sweet-tart flesh. *Friar* and *Queen Anne* plums are related to the Santa Rosa and have similar qualities. *Wild plums* are small and grow in bunches and are primarily used to make jams and jellies. When cooked, the amount of sugar needed will depend on the variety.

Polynesian Drumsticks

A quick marinade adds a sweet and tangy glaze to grilled skinless drumsticks—a favorite with everyone in the family.

PREP 15 minutes plus marinating   **GRILL** 25 minutes   **MAKES** 4 main-dish servings.

1 can (8 ounces) crushed pineapple in unsweetened pineapple juice

1/4 cup packed brown sugar

3 tablespoons soy sauce

1 tablespoon grated, peeled fresh ginger

1 garlic clove, crushed with garlic press

12 large chicken drumsticks (4 pounds), skin removed

1. In blender, puree pineapple and its juice, brown sugar, soy sauce, ginger, and garlic. Spoon 1/2 cup pineapple mixture into large ziptight plastic bag; reserve remaining pineapple mixture for grilling. Add drumsticks to bag, turning to coat. Let stand at room temperature 15 minutes.

2. Remove drumsticks from bag; discard bag with marinade. Place drumsticks on hot grill rack over medium heat and grill, turning once, 15 minutes. Grill, brushing twice with reserved pineapple mixture and turning occasionally, until drumsticks are golden and juices run clear when thickest part is pierced with tip of knife, 10 to 15 minutes longer.

EACH SERVING About 260 calories | 38g protein | 8g carbohydrate | 8g total fat (2g saturated) | 123mg cholesterol | 385mg sodium.

Basic Chicken Burgers

If you're looking for plain, straightforward burgers, we've got them. We also have suggestions to jazz them up to please a variety of cravings, so pick your favorite flavor family: teriyaki, barbecue, or herb.

PREP 20 minutes **GRILL** 12 minutes **MAKES** 4 main-dish servings.

I pound ground chicken meat

I medium carrot, peeled and grated ($\frac{1}{2}$ cup)

2 green onions, trimmed and minced

I garlic clove, crushed with garlic press

4 hamburger buns, warmed

sliced cucumber, lettuce leaves, and green onion (optional)

1. Prepare grill. In medium bowl, with hands, mix ground chicken, carrot, green onions, and garlic until evenly combined.

2. On waxed paper, shape chicken mixture into four $3\frac{1}{2}$-inch round patties (mixture will be very soft and moist), handling meat as little as possible.

3. Place patties on hot grill rack over medium heat and grill, turning once, until juices run clear when center of burger is pierced with tip of knife, about 12 minutes. (If you have a grill with widely spaced grates, you may want to place burgers on a perforated grill topper to keep them intact.)

4. Place burgers on warmed buns. Serve with cucumber slices, lettuce leaves, and green onions if you like.

EACH SERVING About 275 calories | 30g protein | 24g carbohydrate | 5g total fat (1g saturated) | 72mg cholesterol | 310mg sodium.

Teriyaki Burgers

Before shaping into patties, combine *2 tablespoons soy sauce, 1 tablespoon seasoned rice vinegar, 2 teaspoons grated, peeled fresh ginger,* and *2 teaspoons Asian sesame oil* with ground chicken mixture just until well blended but not overmixed. (Prepare burger mixture just before cooking to prevent ginger from changing texture of meat.) Grill as directed.

EACH SERVING About 305 calories | 31g protein | 26g carbohydrate | 8g total fat (2g saturated) | 72mg cholesterol | 940mg sodium.

Barbecue Burgers

Before shaping into patties, combine *2 tablespoons chili sauce, 1 tablespoon light (mild) molasses, 2 teaspoons cayenne pepper sauce, 2 teaspoons Worcestershire sauce,* and *1/4 teaspoon salt* with ground chicken mixture just until well blended but not overmixed. Grill as directed.

EACH SERVING About 295 calories | 31g protein | 30g carbohydrate | 5g total fat (1g saturated) | 72mg cholesterol | 715mg sodium.

Herb Burgers

Before shaping into patties, combine *2 tablespoons finely chopped fresh dill, 1 tablespoon dried mint, 1 tablespoon fresh lemon juice, 1 teaspoon ground cumin, 1/2 teaspoon salt,* and *1/8 teaspoon ground red pepper (cayenne)* with ground chicken mixture just until well blended but not overmixed. Grill as directed.

EACH SERVING About 280 calories | 31g protein | 25g carbohydrate | 5g total fat (1g saturated) | 72mg cholesterol | 605mg sodium.

Soups,
Salads &
Sandwiches

Baby Spinach with Nectarines and Grilled Chicken
recipe on page 165

Vietnamese Noodle Soup

Pho, the classic Vietnamese soup, is typically served with thin slices of beef, but our version is made with chicken.

PREP 20 minutes   **COOK** 25 minutes   **MAKES** 4 main-dish servings.

4 ounces flat dried rice noodles or linguine

7 cups low-sodium chicken broth

6 sprigs basil

6 sprigs cilantro

1 teaspoon coriander seeds

1 cinnamon stick (3 inches long)

2 garlic cloves, peeled

3 green onions, trimmed and thinly sliced diagonally

1 pound skinless, boneless chicken breast halves, cut into thin diagonal strips

4 medium mushrooms, trimmed and sliced

fresh cilantro leaves and lime wedges (optional)

1. In large bowl, soak rice noodles in enough *warm water* to cover for 20 minutes. Drain noodles.

2. Meanwhile, in 3-quart saucepan, heat broth, basil, cilantro, coriander seeds, cinnamon stick, garlic, and one-third of green onions to boiling over high heat. Reduce heat to low; cover and simmer 10 minutes. Strain broth through sieve; discard solids and return broth to saucepan.

3. Stir chicken, mushrooms, drained noodles, and remaining green onions into broth; heat to boiling over high heat. Reduce heat to low; cover and simmer until chicken loses its pink color throughout, about 3 minutes. Serve with fresh cilantro leaves and lime wedges, if you like.

EACH SERVING About 255 calories | **32g protein** | **26g carbohydrate** | **2g total fat (0g saturated)** | **66mg cholesterol** | **1,110mg sodium.**

South-of-the-Border Chicken Soup

If corn on the cob is available, cut the kernels from four ears and use instead of the canned corn.

PREP 25 minutes **COOK** I hour **MAKES** 8 main-dish servings.

8 medium all-purpose potatoes (2½ pounds)

10 cups water

1 chicken (4 pounds), cut into 8 pieces

3 large stalks celery, cut into thirds

3 carrots, peeled and cut into thirds

2 medium onions, not peeled, cut into quarters

10 sprigs plus ¼ cup chopped fresh cilantro

2 bay leaves

1 teaspoon whole black peppercorns

1 can (15¼ to 16 ounces) whole-kernel corn, drained

2 teaspoons salt

¼ cup fresh lime juice (2 large limes)

2 ripe medium avocados, pitted, peeled, cut into ½-inch pieces

tortilla chips

lime wedges

1. Peel 3 potatoes. In 8-quart Dutch oven, combine water, chicken, peeled potatoes, celery, carrots, onions, cilantro sprigs, bay leaves, and peppercorns; heat to boiling over high heat. Reduce heat; cover and simmer until chicken loses its pink color throughout and vegetables are tender, 35 to 45 minutes. Transfer chicken and potatoes to separate bowls.

2. Strain broth through sieve into large bowl; discard vegetables. Skim and discard fat from broth; return broth to same clean Dutch oven. Mash cooked potatoes with 1 cup broth; stir mashed-potato mixture into broth in Dutch oven.

3. Peel and chop remaining 5 potatoes. Add potatoes to broth; heat to boiling over high heat. Reduce heat; cover and simmer until potatoes are tender, about 10 minutes.

4. Meanwhile, discard skin and bones from chicken; cut chicken into bite-size pieces. Stir chicken, corn, and salt into broth; heat through.

5. Just before serving, stir lime juice and chopped cilantro into soup. Serve with avocado, tortilla chips, and lime wedges.

EACH SERVING WITHOUT GARNISHES About 344 calories | 28g protein | 34g carbohydrate | 12g total fat (2g saturated) | 76mg cholesterol | 772mg sodium.

Chicken Soup with Rice

For an Italian touch, add thinly sliced spinach leaves and sprinkle each serving with freshly grated Parmesan cheese.

PREP 10 minutes plus preparation of broth   **COOK** 30 minutes
MAKES about 6½ cups or 6 first-course servings.

5 cups low-sodium chicken broth

3 carrots, peeled and cut into ¼-inch pieces

1 stalk celery, cut into ¼-inch pieces

1 teaspoon salt

2 cups bite-size pieces cooked chicken (9 ounces)

1 cup regular long-grain rice or ¾ cup small pasta shapes, such as tubettini, alphabets, stars, or orzo, cooked as label directs

1. Remove and discard fat from broth.

2. In 3-quart saucepan, combine carrots, celery, broth, and salt; heat to boiling over high heat. Reduce heat and simmer until vegetables are very tender, about 15 minutes. Stir in chicken and rice; heat through.

EACH SERVING About 203 calories | 18g protein | 22g carbohydrate | 5g total fat (2g saturated) | 44mg cholesterol | 523mg sodium.

Homemade Chicken Broth

Nothing beats the flavor of homemade chicken broth. Make it in large batches and freeze in sturdy containers for up to three months. Our recipe has an added bonus: The cooked chicken can be used in casseroles and salads.

PREP 10 minutes plus cooling   **COOK** 4 hours 30 minutes   **MAKES** about 5 cups.

I chicken (3 to 3¹/₂ pounds), including neck (giblets reserved for another use)

2 carrots, peeled and cut into 2-inch pieces

I stalk celery, cut into 2-inch pieces

I medium onion, cut into quarters

5 parsley sprigs

I garlic clove

¹/₂ teaspoon dried thyme

¹/₂ bay leaf

1. In 6-quart saucepot, combine chicken, chicken neck, carrots, celery, onion, parsley, garlic, thyme, bay leaf, and enough *water* to cover; heat to boiling over high heat. Skim foam from surface. Reduce heat and simmer, turning chicken once and skimming, 1 hour.

2. Remove from heat; transfer chicken to large bowl. When cool enough to handle, remove skin and bones from chicken. (Reserve chicken for another use.) Return skin and bones to Dutch oven and heat to boiling; skim foam. Reduce heat and simmer 3 hours.

3. Strain broth through colander into large bowl; discard solids. Strain again through sieve into containers; cool. Cover and refrigerate to use within 3 days, or freeze up to 4 months.

4. To use, skim and discard fat from surface of broth.

EACH CUP About 36 calories | 3g protein | 4g carbohydrate | 1g total fat (1g saturated) | 3mg cholesterol | 91mg sodium.

Cajun Chicken Salad with Green Grapes

Green grapes and sweet red peppers balance the spicy dressing of this zesty salad.

PREP 25 minutes **COOK** 20 minutes **MAKES** 8 main-dish servings.

I lemon, thinly sliced

I bay leaf

$^1/_2$ teaspoon whole black peppercorns

$^1/_2$ teaspoon dried thyme

6 medium skinless, boneless chicken breast halves ($1^3/_4$ pounds)

$^3/_4$ teaspoon paprika

$^1/_3$ cup light mayonnaise

$^1/_3$ cup reduced-fat sour cream

$^3/_4$ teaspoon salt

$^1/_4$ teaspoon coarsely ground black pepper

$^1/_8$ teaspoon ground nutmeg

3 cups green grapes (12 ounces), each cut in half

I large red pepper, cut into $^1/_2$-inch pieces

$^1/_2$ cup loosely packed fresh parsley leaves, chopped

$^1/_4$ cup thinly sliced red onion

I large pickled jalapeño chile, minced

1. In 12-inch skillet, heat *1 inch water* with lemon slices, bay leaf, peppercorns, and $^1/_4$ teaspoon thyme to boiling over high heat. Add chicken; reduce heat to low and simmer, turning chicken halfway through cooking, until chicken just loses its pink color throughout, 12 to 14 minutes. With slotted spoon or tongs, transfer chicken to cutting board; set aside until cool enough to handle. Cut chicken into $^3/_4$-inch pieces.

2. Discard poaching liquid and wipe skillet dry. Add paprika and remaining $^1/_4$ teaspoon thyme to skillet; toast over medium-low heat, stirring, 2 minutes.

3. Transfer paprika mixture to large bowl; stir in mayonnaise, sour cream, salt, ground pepper, and nutmeg until blended. Add chicken, grapes, red pepper, parsley, onion, and jalapeño; toss until evenly coated. Serve salad warm, or cover and refrigerate until ready to serve.

EACH SERVING About 200 calories I 24g protein I 16g carbohydrate I 4g total fat (1g saturated) I 64mg cholesterol I 380mg sodium.

Chinese Chicken Salad

We dressed this salad with an Asian-inspired vinaigrette made with fresh orange juice for delicious citrus flavor.

PREP 25 minutes   **COOK** 10 minutes   **MAKES** 4 main-dish servings.

CITRUS VINAIGRETTE

1 medium orange

3 tablespoons seasoned rice vinegar

3 tablespoons soy sauce

1 tablespoon Asian sesame oil

1 teaspoon sugar

1 teaspoon grated, peeled
   fresh ginger

CHICKEN SALAD

1 package (10 ounces) shredded
   carrots

1 tablespoon vegetable oil

1 pound skinless, boneless chicken
   breasts, cut into $3/4$-inch pieces

2 garlic cloves, crushed with
   garlic press

2 teaspoons grated, peeled
   fresh ginger

2 bunches watercress (6 ounces
   each), tough stems discarded

2 green onions, trimmed and sliced

1 tablespoon toasted sesame seeds

1. Prepare vinaigrette: From orange, grate 1 teaspoon peel and squeeze $1/4$ cup juice. In small bowl, with wire whisk or fork, mix orange peel and juice with rice vinegar, soy sauce, sesame oil, sugar, and ginger; set aside.

2. Prepare chicken salad: In nonstick 12-inch skillet, place carrots; add enough *water* to cover and heat to boiling over high heat. Reduce heat to low; simmer 1 minute. Rinse carrots with cold water to stop cooking; drain well. Transfer carrots to large salad bowl. Wipe skillet dry.

3. In same skillet, heat vegetable oil over medium-high heat until hot. Add chicken and cook, stirring frequently (stir-frying), 5 minutes. Add garlic and ginger and stir-fry until chicken loses its pink color throughout, 1 to 3 minutes longer. Transfer chicken mixture to bowl with carrots.

4. Add vinaigrette, watercress, and green onions to bowl with carrots; toss to combine. Sprinkle salad with sesame seeds.

EACH SERVING About 280 calories | 30g protein | 18g carbohydrate | 10g total fat (1g saturated) | 66mg cholesterol | 1,215mg sodium.

Grilled Chicken Taco Salad

A great way to prepare a Mexican favorite during the summer: Spicy chicken cutlets are grilled, then served over black-bean salsa, shredded lettuce, and crisp corn tortillas.

PREP 25 minutes **GRILL** 10 minutes **MAKES** 4 main-dish servings.

1 can (15 to 19 ounces) black beans, rinsed and drained

3/4 cup medium-hot jarred salsa

1 tablespoon fresh lime juice

1 cup loosely packed fresh cilantro leaves, chopped

2 tablespoons chili powder

1 teaspoon ground cumin

1 teaspoon ground coriander

1 teaspoon brown sugar

1/2 teaspoon salt

1/4 teaspoon ground red pepper (cayenne)

1 tablespoon olive oil

1 pound chicken cutlets

4 corn tortillas

4 cups thinly sliced iceberg lettuce

lime wedges, avocado slices, and sour cream (optional)

1. Prepare grill. In medium bowl, mix beans, salsa, lime juice, and half of cilantro; set aside.

2. In cup, stir chili powder, cumin, coriander, sugar, salt, ground red pepper, and oil until evenly mixed (mixture will be dry).

3. If necessary, pound cutlets to uniform 1/4-inch thickness. With hands, rub chicken with chili-powder mixture.

4. Place chicken on hot grill rack over medium-high heat and cook, turning once, until chicken loses its pink color throughout, 8 to 10 minutes. Place corn tortillas on grill with chicken and cook, turning once, until lightly browned, 3 to 5 minutes. Transfer chicken to cutting board. Place tortillas on 4 dinner plates.

5. Slice chicken into long, thin strips. Top tortillas with lettuce, bean mixture, and chicken strips. Sprinkle with remaining cilantro. If you like, serve with lime wedges, avocado slices, and sour cream.

EACH SERVING About 370 calories | 35g protein | 45g carbohydrate | 8g total fat (2g saturated) | 72mg cholesterol | 1,075mg sodium.

Curried Chicken-Mango Salad

Precooked chicken from the deli or supermarket makes our salad a cinch. The recipe can easily be doubled if you need to feed a crowd.

PREP 20 minutes   **MAKES** 4 main-dish servings.

I store-bought rotisserie chicken (2 pounds)

$1/4$ cup plain lowfat yogurt

$1/4$ cup light mayonnaise

2 tablespoons mango chutney, chopped

I tablespoon fresh lime juice

I teaspoon curry powder

I ripe large mango, peeled and diced

I medium stalk celery, diced

I medium Granny Smith apple, cored and diced

$1/2$ cup loosely packed fresh cilantro leaves, chopped

I head leaf lettuce, separated and rinsed

I. Remove skin from chicken; discard. With fingers, pull chicken meat into 1-inch pieces. (You should have about 3 cups, or about $3/4$ pound meat.)

2. In large bowl, mix yogurt, mayonnaise, chutney, lime juice, and curry powder until combined. Stir in chicken, mango, celery, apple, and cilantro until well coated. Serve salad on bed of lettuce leaves.

EACH SERVING About 310 calories | **32g protein** | **25g carbohydrate** | **9g total fat (2g saturated)** | **95mg cholesterol** | **255mg sodium.**

Curried Chicken with Mango and Cantaloupe Slaw

A cooling toss of melon and mango makes a perfect partner for this spicy grilled chicken.

PREP 5 minutes plus marinating   **GRILL** 10 minutes   **MAKES** 4 main-dish servings.

1 to 2 limes

1 container (6 ounces) plain lowfat yogurt

3/4 teaspoon curry powder

2 tablespoons chopped crystallized ginger

1 teaspoon salt

1/4 teaspoon crushed red pepper

4 medium skinless, boneless chicken breast halves (1 1/4 pounds)

1/2 small cantaloupe, rind removed, and cut into julienne strips (2 cups)

1 large mango, peeled and cut into julienne strips (2 cups)

1/2 cup loosely packed fresh cilantro leaves, chopped

1 head Boston lettuce

lime wedges (optional)

1. From limes, grate 1/2 teaspoon peel and squeeze 2 tablespoons juice. In large bowl, whisk 1 tablespoon lime juice and 1/4 teaspoon lime peel with yogurt, curry powder, 2 tablespoons ginger, 3/4 teaspoon salt, and 1/8 teaspoon crushed red pepper until blended. Add chicken, turning to coat with marinade. Cover and let stand, turning occasionally, 15 minutes at room temperature or 30 minutes in refrigerator.

2. Meanwhile, prepare slaw: In medium bowl, with rubber spatula, gently stir cantaloupe, mango, cilantro, remaining 2 tablespoons ginger, 1 tablespoon lime juice, 1/4 teaspoon lime peel, 1/4 teaspoon salt, and 1/8 teaspoon crushed red pepper; set aside. Makes about 4 cups.

3. Lightly grease grill rack. Prepare grill.

4. Remove chicken from marinade; discard marinade. Arrange chicken on hot grill rack over medium heat and grill, covered, or turning once, until chicken loses its pink color throughout, 10 to 12 minutes. Transfer to cutting board. When cool enough to handle, cut into long, thin slices.

5. To serve, arrange lettuce leaves on 4 dinner plates; top with chicken and slaw. Serve with lime wedges, if you like.

EACH SERVING CHICKEN WITH LETTUCE About 205 calories | 34g protein | 5g carbohydrate | 4g total fat (1g saturated) | 92mg cholesterol | 330mg sodium.

EACH ¹/₂ CUP SLAW About 50 calories | 1g protein | 13g carbohydrate | 0g total fat | 0mg cholesterol | 150mg sodium.

Cutting a Mango

With a sharp knife, cut a lengthwise slice from each side of the long flat seed, as close to the seed as possible. Peel seed section; cut off as much flesh as possible; discard seed.

Cut the mango pieces lengthwise into thick wedges. Use a knife to remove the peel from each wedge, cutting close to the peel.

For eating mango out of hand, score the flesh of each piece without cutting through the skin, and gently push it out to eat.

Grilled Chicken and Pepper Salad

A great summer salad combo—grilled chicken breasts, peppers, and onions all tossed in a tangy balsamic vinaigrette with peppery arugula leaves.

PREP 15 minutes **GRILL** 20 minutes **MAKES** 4 main-dish servings.

BALSAMIC VINAIGRETTE

3 tablespoons olive oil

2 tablespoons balsamic vinegar

1 small garlic clove, crushed with garlic press

1 teaspoon Dijon mustard

$1/2$ teaspoon sugar

$1/2$ teaspoon salt

$1/4$ teaspoon coarsely ground black pepper

VEGETABLES AND CHICKEN

2 red peppers

2 yellow peppers

1 large red onion (12 ounces), cut into 8 wedges

4 teaspoons olive oil

1 pound skinless, boneless chicken breast halves

$1/4$ teaspoon salt

$1/4$ teaspoon coarsely ground black pepper

1 cup grape tomatoes

1 bunch arugula (4 ounces), tough stems removed

1. Prepare vinaigrette: In serving bowl, with wire whisk, mix oil, vinegar, garlic, mustard, sugar, salt, and pepper until blended; set aside.

2. Prepare vegetables and chicken: Cut each pepper lengthwise in half; discard stems and seeds. With hand, flatten each pepper half. In bowl, toss peppers and onion wedges with 3 teaspoons oil. Rub chicken breasts with remaining 1 teaspoon oil; sprinkle with salt and pepper.

3. Place chicken on hot grill rack over medium heat and grill, turning once, until chicken loses its pink color throughout, 12 to 15 minutes.

4. While chicken is cooking, place onion wedges and peppers, skin side down, on same grill. Cook onion, turning occasionally, until golden, about

15 minutes; cook peppers until skins are charred and blistered, 18 to 20 minutes.

5. When onion wedges are done, transfer to plate. When chicken is done, transfer to cutting board. When peppers are done, wrap in foil and allow them to steam at room temperature until cool enough to handle, about 10 minutes.

6. While peppers are steaming, slice chicken breasts crosswise into ½-inch-wide strips.

7. Remove peppers from foil; discard skins. Thinly slice peppers. Add peppers, chicken, onion, tomatoes, and arugula to bowl with dressing; toss gently to coat.

EACH SERVING **About 330 calories | 29g protein | 18g carbohydrate | 16g total fat (3g saturated) | 72mg cholesterol | 520mg sodium.**

Chicken Salad with Croutons and Lemon-Caper Vinaigrette

Turn ordinary chicken salad into something sublime with homemade garlic-flavored croutons and a creamy lemon vinaigrette.

PREP 30 minutes   **COOK** 15 minutes   **MAKES** 4 main-dish servings.

$1/2$ medium head chicory (8 ounces), torn into 2-inch pieces

I medium head radicchio (6 ounces), cut into $1/2$-inch slices

I medium head Belgian endive (6 ounces), cut into thin lengthwise strips

3 tablespoons butter or margarine

$1/2$ long loaf (8 ounces) Italian bread, cut into 1-inch cubes

I garlic clove, sliced

4 small skinless, boneless chicken breast halves (I pound)

$1/2$ teaspoon salt

I large lemon

2 tablespoons capers, drained and chopped

2 teaspoons Dijon mustard

I teaspoon sugar

$1/4$ teaspoon coarsely ground black pepper

3 tablespoons olive oil

1. Place chicory, radicchio, and Belgian endive in large bowl.

2. In nonstick 12-inch skillet, melt 2 tablespoons butter over medium heat. Add bread cubes and garlic and cook, stirring occasionally, until bread is lightly browned. Discard garlic; transfer garlic croutons to bowl with salad greens. Wipe skillet clean.

3. Add remaining 1 tablespoon butter to skillet. Add chicken and $1/4$ teaspoon salt and cook until chicken is browned on both sides. Reduce heat to medium; cover and cook until chicken loses its pink color throughout, about 6 to 8 minutes longer. Transfer chicken to plate.

4. From lemon, grate 1 teaspoon peel and squeeze 2 tablespoons juice. In small bowl, combine lemon juice, lemon peel, capers, mustard, sugar, pepper, remaining $1/4$ teaspoon salt, and any juices from plate with chicken. In thin, steady stream, whisk in oil until mixture thickens slightly.

5. Toss salad greens and garlic croutons with three-fourths of dressing. Arrange salad on 4 dinner plates; top with chicken and drizzle with remaining dressing.

EACH SERVING About 485 calories | 33g protein | 37g carbohydrate | 22g total fat (8g saturated) | 89mg cholesterol | 1,058mg sodium.

Chicken-Spinach Salad with Warm Mushroom and Onion Vinaigrette

This elegant main-dish salad is a snap to prepare with packaged sliced mushrooms and a rotisserie chicken.

PREP 10 minutes **COOK** 15 minutes **MAKES** 4 main-dish servings.

3 tablespoons olive oil

I large red onion, cut in half and thinly sliced

$^1/_2$ teaspoon salt

$^1/_4$ teaspoon coarsely ground black pepper

2 packages (4 ounces each) assorted sliced wild mushrooms (gourmet blend)

$^1/_3$ cup cider vinegar

I tablespoon sugar

2 bags (5 to 6 ounces each) baby spinach

2 cups ($^1/_2$-inch pieces) rotisserie chicken meat (10 ounces)

1. In nonstick 12-inch skillet, heat 1 tablespoon oil over medium-high heat until hot. Add onion, salt, and pepper, and cook, stirring occasionally, until onion is tender and golden, about 10 minutes. Add mushrooms and cook until mushrooms are browned and liquid has evaporated, about 5 minutes.

2. Stir vinegar, sugar, and remaining 2 tablespoons oil into mushroom mixture; heat to boiling. Boil, stirring, 30 seconds.

3. In large serving bowl, toss spinach and chicken with warm dressing until salad is evenly coated. Serve immediately.

EACH SERVING About 280 calories | 25g protein | 11g carbohydrate | 16g total fat (3g saturated) | 62mg cholesterol | 455mg sodium.

Baby Spinach with Nectarines and Grilled Chicken

There's no waste with baby spinach; it's so tender, you can eat it stems and all.

PREP 25 minutes   **GRILL** 15 minutes   **MAKES** 4 main-dish servings.

I pound skinless, boneless chicken breast halves

I teaspoon fresh thyme leaves

$3/4$ teaspoon salt

$1/2$ teaspoon coarsely ground black pepper

2 tablespoons olive oil

I tablespoon balsamic vinegar

$1/2$ teaspoon Dijon mustard

I shallot, minced

2 large ripe nectarines, pitted and sliced

$1/2$ English (seedless) cucumber, cut lengthwise in half, then thinly sliced crosswise

8 ounces baby spinach

2 ounces crumbled feta cheese ($1/2$ cup)

1. Prepare grill. Rub chicken with thyme, $1/2$ teaspoon salt, and $1/4$ teaspoon pepper.

2. Arrange chicken on hot grill rack over medium heat and grill, turning once, until chicken loses its pink color throughout, about 7 minutes per side. Transfer chicken to cutting board; set aside until cool enough to handle.

3. Meanwhile, in large bowl, with wire whisk, mix oil, vinegar, mustard, shallot, remaining $1/4$ teaspoon salt, and remaining $1/4$ teaspoon pepper. Stir in nectarines and cucumber.

4. To serve, cut chicken into $1/2$-inch-thick slices. Toss spinach with nectarine mixture. Arrange salad on 4 plates; top with feta and sliced chicken.

EACH SERVING About 285 calories | 31g protein | 15g carbohydrate | 12g total fat (3g saturated) | 78mg cholesterol | 730mg sodium.

Warm and Spicy
Asian Chicken Salad

A quick sauté of gingery chicken and Asian vegetables top a tangy salad of Napa cabbage. For a touch of nostalgia, add some fried Chinese noodles.

PREP 15 minutes **COOK** 25 minutes **MAKES** 4 main-dish servings.

4 tablespoons soy sauce

I tablespoon minced, peeled
   fresh ginger

³/₄ teaspoon crushed red pepper

I garlic clove, minced

I¹/₂ pounds skinless, boneless
   chicken breasts, cut into
   bite-size pieces

¹/₂ pound bean sprouts

2 tablespoons plus ¹/₄ cup
   vegetable oil

¹/₂ pound snow peas, strings
   removed

4 ounces fresh shiitake mushrooms,
   stems discarded and caps sliced

I can (8 ounces) sliced water
   chestnuts, rinsed and drained

2 tablespoons white wine vinegar

2 teaspoons sugar

¹/₂ teaspoon dry mustard

¹/₂ small head **Napa (Chinese)**
   cabbage, (12 ounces), thinly sliced

1. In medium bowl, combine 2 tablespoons soy sauce, ginger, crushed red pepper, and garlic. Add chicken; stir to coat.

2. In separate bowl, place bean sprouts. Add enough *boiling water* to cover; let stand 5 minutes. Drain.

3. In nonstick 10-inch skillet, heat 1 tablespoon oil over medium-high heat. Add snow peas and shiitake mushrooms and cook until snow peas are tender-crisp and mushrooms are tender, about 5 minutes. With slotted spoon, transfer to large bowl.

4. Add 1 tablespoon vegetable oil to skillet. Add chicken, half at a time, and cook until chicken is golden brown on the outside and just loses its pink color throughout, about 5 minutes. Add chicken and water chestnuts to snow-pea mixture.

5. In small bowl, with wire whisk or fork, mix vinegar, sugar, dry mustard, remaining $1/4$ cup oil, and remaining 2 tablespoons soy sauce. Add dressing to chicken mixture; toss to mix well.

6. To serve, toss Napa cabbage with bean sprouts. Arrange Napa mixture on large platter; top with chicken mixture.

EACH SERVING About 470 calories | 46g protein | 20g carbohydrate | 23g total fat (3g saturated) | 99mg cholesterol | 1,155mg sodium.

Italian Chicken Sandwiches

This delicious sandwich gets its great flavor from mayonnaise that is blended with arugula and Parmesan cheese. For the finishing touch, the chicken is topped with roasted red peppers.

PREP 10 minutes **COOK** 15 minutes **MAKES** 6 sandwiches.

1 small bunch arugula, trimmed (1 1/2 cups loosely packed)

1/2 cup mayonnaise

1/4 cup freshly grated Parmesan or Romano cheese

1/2 teaspoon salt

3/4 teaspoon coarsely ground black pepper

2 tablespoons all-purpose flour

6 large skinless, boneless chicken breast halves (2 1/4 pounds)

2 tablespoons olive oil

6 large sandwich rolls

1 small head leaf lettuce, separated into leaves

1 jar (10 to 12 ounces) roasted red peppers, drained

1. In blender or in food processor with knife blade attached, process arugula, mayonnaise, Parmesan, 1/4 teaspoon salt, and 1/4 teaspoon pepper until arugula is finely chopped; set mixture aside.

2. On waxed paper, mix flour, remaining 1/4 teaspoon salt, and remaining 1/2 teaspoon pepper; use to coat chicken breasts.

3. In 12-inch skillet, heat oil over medium-high heat until very hot. Add chicken and cook, turning once, until chicken loses its pink color throughout, about 15 minutes.

4. To serve, slice each chicken breast horizontally in half. Slice each sandwich roll horizontally in half. Top bottom halves of rolls with lettuce leaves, sautéed chicken breasts, then roasted red peppers. Spread arugula mixture on top halves of sandwich rolls.

EACH SANDWICH About 660 calories | 49g protein | 51g carbohydrate | 29g total fat (6g saturated) | 114mg cholesterol | 1,000mg sodium.

Spicy Guacamole and Chicken Roll-Ups

To make the filling for this wrap, the chicken is cooked, cooled, and then "pulled" into shreds—a technique used most often with pork. For added zest, the tortillas are spread with a spicy guacamole—it's great with tortilla chips, too.

PREP 30 minutes   **COOK** 15 minutes   **MAKES** 4 sandwiches.

2 teaspoons olive oil

1 pound skinless, boneless chicken breast halves

1/2 teaspoon salt

1/2 teaspoon coarsely ground black pepper

2 medium avocados (8 ounces each), pitted, peeled, and cut into small chunks

1 medium tomato, diced

1/4 cup loosely packed fresh cilantro leaves, coarsely chopped

4 teaspoons fresh lime juice

2 teaspoons finely chopped red onion

1 teaspoon adobo sauce from canned chipotle chiles or 2 tablespoons chipotle pepper sauce

4 (10-inch) flour tortillas, warmed

2 cups sliced iceberg lettuce

1. In 10-inch skillet, heat oil over medium-high heat until very hot. Add chicken and sprinkle with 1/4 teaspoon salt and 1/4 teaspoon pepper. Cook chicken, turning once, until chicken loses its pink color throughout, about 12 minutes. Transfer chicken to plate; set aside until cool enough to handle, about 5 minutes.

2. Meanwhile, in medium bowl, with rubber spatula, gently stir avocados, tomato, cilantro, lime juice, red onion, adobo sauce, and remaining 1/4 teaspoon salt and 1/4 teaspoon pepper until blended.

3. Pull chicken into thin shreds. Place tortillas on work surface; spread with guacamole. Place chicken, then lettuce on top of guacamole. Roll tortillas around filling.

EACH SANDWICH About 475 calories | 33g protein | 40g carbohydrate | 21g total fat (3g saturated) | 66mg cholesterol | 745mg sodium.

Index

Photography Credits

Page 4: Ann Stratton **Page 6:** Mark Thomas **Page 11:** Alan Richardson **Page 15:** Brian Hagiwara **Page 17:** Rita Maas **Page 21:** Brian Hagiwara **Page 28:** Brian Hagiwara **Page 31:** Alan Richardson **Page 33:** Ann Stratton **Page 35:** Brian Hagiwara **Page 37:** Brian Hagiwara **Page 41:** Brian Hagiwara **Page 43:** Brian Hagiwara **Page 55:** Mark Thomas **Page 57:** Alan Richardson **Page 60:** Mark Thomas **Page 65:** Lisa Koenig **Page 69:** Brian Hagiwara **Page 71:** Rita Maas **Page 77:** Rita Maas **Page 85:** Brian Hagiwara **Page 87:** Brian Hagiwara **Page 89:** Ann Stratton **Page 95:** Ann Stratton **Page 96:** Ann Stratton **Page 99:** Brian Hagiwara **Page 100:** Brian Hagiwara **Page 103:** Rita Maas **Page 106:** Brian Hagiwara **Page 117:** Lisa Koenig **Page 119:** Brian Hagiwara **Page 125:** Alan Richardson **Page 127:** Mark Thomas **Page 128:** Brian Hagiwara **Page 131:** Brian Hagiwara **Page 133:** Brian Hagiwara **Page 141:** Ann Stratton **Page 142:** Alan Richardson **Page 144:** Alan Richardson **Page 147:** Ann Stratton **Page 149:** Mark Thomas **Page 151:** Ann Stratton **Page 159:** Ann Stratton **Page 161:** Alan Richardson **Page 163:** Lisa Koenig

Metric Conversion Chart

The recipes that appear in this cookbook use the standard United States method for measuring liquid and dry or solid ingredients (teaspoons, tablespoons, and cups). The information on this chart is provided to help cooks outside the U.S. successfully use these recipes. All equivalents are approximate.

Metric Equivalents for Different Types of Ingredients

A standard cup measure of a dry or solid ingredient will vary in weight depending on the type of ingredient. A standard cup of liquid is the same volume for any type of liquid. Use the following chart when converting standard cup measures to grams (weight) or milliliters (volume).

Standard Cup	Fine Powder (e.g. flour)	Grain (e.g. rice)	Granular (e.g. sugar)	Liquid Solids (e.g. butter)	Liquid (e.g. milk)
1	140 g	150 g	190 g	200 g	240 ml
3/4	105 g	113 g	143 g	150 g	180 ml
2/3	93 g	100 g	125 g	133 g	160 ml
1/2	70 g	75 g	95 g	100 g	120 ml
1/3	47 g	50 g	63 g	67 g	80 ml
1/4	35 g	38 g	48 g	50 g	60 ml
1/8	18 g	19 g	24 g	25 g	30 ml

Useful Equivalents for Liquid Ingredients By Volume

1/4 tsp	=					1 ml
1/2 tsp	=					2 ml
1 tsp	=					5 ml
3 tsp	=	1 tbls =		1/2 fl oz	=	15 ml
		2 tbls =	1/8 cup	1 fl oz	=	30 ml
		4 tbls =	1/4 cup	2 fl oz	=	60 ml
		5 1/3 tbls =	1/3 cup	3 fl oz	=	80 ml
		8 tbls =	1/2 cup	4 fl oz	=	120 ml
		10 2/3 tbls =	2/3 cup	5 fl oz	=	160 ml
		12 tbls =	3/4 cup	6 fl oz	=	180 ml
		16 tbls =	1 cup	8 fl oz	=	240 ml
		1 pt =	2 cups	16 fl oz	=	480 ml
		1 qt =	4 cups	32 fl oz	=	960 ml
				33 fl oz	=	1000 ml = 1l

Useful Equivalents for Cooking/Oven Temperatures

	Fahrenheit	Celsius	Gas Mark
Freeze Water	32° F	0° C	
Room Temperature	68° F	20° C	
Boil Water	212° F	100° C	
Bake	325° F	160° C	3
	350° F	180° C	4
	375° F	190° C	5
	400° F	200° C	6
	425° F	220° C	7
	450° F	230° C	8
Broil			Grill

Useful Equivalents For Dry Ingredients By Weight

(To convert ounces to grams, multiply the number of ounces by 30.)

1 oz	=	1/16 lb	=	30 g
4 oz	=	1/4 lb	=	120 g
8 oz	=	1/2 lb	=	240 g
12 oz	=	3/4 lb	=	360 g
16 oz	=	1 lb	=	480 g

Useful Equivalents for Length

(To convert inches to centimeters, multiply the number of inches by 2.5.)

1 in	=		2.5 cm
6 in	=	1/2 ft =	15 cm
12 in	=	1 ft =	30 cm
36 in	=	3 ft = 1 yd =	90 cm
40 in	=		100 cm = 1 m